THE
SECRET LIFE
OF MONEY

THE
SECRET LIFE
OF MONEY

EVERYDAY ECONOMICS EXPLAINED

DANIEL DAVIES AND TESS READ

metro

Published by Metro Publishing
an imprint of John Blake Publishing Ltd,
3 Bramber Court, 2 Bramber Road,
London W14 9PB, England

www.johnblakepublishing.co.uk

www.facebook.com/johnblakebooks ￼
twitter.com/jblakebooks ￼

This edition published in 2015

ISBN: 978 1 78219 995 3

British Library Cataloguing-in-Publication Data:

A catalogue record for this book is available from the British Library.

Design by www.envydesign.co.uk

Printed in Great Britain by CPI Group (UK) Ltd

1 3 5 7 9 10 8 6 4 2

Papers used by John Blake Publishing are natural, recyclable products made
from wood grown in sustainable forests. The manufacturing processes
conform to the environmental regulations of the country of origin.

Every attempt has been made to contact the relevant copyright-holders,
but some were unobtainable. We would be grateful if the appropriate people
could contact us.

CONTENTS

INTRODUCTION

THE SECRETS OF MONEY

People have been complaining to economists about something for decades, but with no apparent effect: it would seem reasonable to suppose that, if you took a degree in economics, or read an introductory economics textbook, you'd come away with a reasonable understanding of how the modern economy worked. At the very least you would expect that someone with an economics degree would understand how businesses worked better than someone without one.

But that is very often just not the case. As the authors of this book, we have worked in management consultancy and investment banking for years, and repeatedly met economics graduates who don't have a clue. (Between us, we have an undergraduate degree in economics, economics training from a world-leading economics specialist university and a postgraduate degree from a prestigious business school.) They weren't much use in understanding what the drivers are in any given business.

THE TROUBLE WITH ECONOMICS

The problem is that the kind of economics they teach in universities is all too abstract. If economists were given the job of writing a textbook on motor vehicle maintenance, they would make sure it started with five chapters explaining the nature of combustion, followed by three chapters explaining the nature of friction. Then they'd have a final chapter showing how a single piston could be made to drive a single crankshaft, some remarks about the need for an electrical system and then they'd send you on your way, telling you that everything from a diesel crane to a Lamborghini was based on the same fundamental principles. Which is true, in a way, but it's not really terribly helpful to someone trying to get their car running, or to understand why their garage bill is so extortionate. What you need to know is the smallest possible set of general principles, but much more about the way in which the various bits fit together.

A LOOK UNDER THE HOOD OF THE MODERN ECONOMY

That's what we're trying to do in this book. Unfortunately, there's no realistic prospect of writing a shop manual for an entire modern industrial economy – it would just be too big, it would take so long that it would be out of date once it was finished, and there is a slight possibility that the readership for it would be somewhat curtailed. But what we think we can do is to give you a bit of a look under the hood; at the way in which things work in some of the bits of the business world that we have come across in our careers. Some of them are large, important parts of the overall economic machine, and some of them are just quirky little micro-industries, but we've selected them on the basis that they all have one or two key characteristics that are seen in a lot of other places. Hopefully, if you look at the things that make, say, the gymnasium industry tick, or what's special about Scotch whisky or payday lending, you'll notice the same kinds of things showing up again in other very different businesses.

THE SECRET LIFE OF MONEY

So, we propose to navigate through the secret life of money, going past whisky distilleries, clothing manufacturers, gyms, pubs and much else besides that forms the essential stuff of life, and emerge enlightened as to what makes all these different types of businesses work. What are the ways in which they make money, and what do these different money-making methods mean to us in our daily lives of interacting with these businesses? How can we better make money work for ourselves once we understand its secret life?

WHY DOES IT COST MORE TO MOVE A PIANO THAN INSTALL A LIFT?

When you move house, if you mention to the removal company that you have a piano that needs to be shifted too – albeit just an upright piano, not a grand piano, let alone a concert piano – the tone of the chat will turn suddenly from friendly to frosty, and the price will shoot vertically upwards. And yet the same does not happen if you own an apartment or office block and speak to a company about a new lift to be installed, which will itself shoot vertically upwards. Why?

Lifts and pianos seem to be similar in that both are bulky, heavy items that are difficult to get round corners and into position correctly, especially if you want them to work properly afterwards. But in business terms they are very different beasts.

ROLLING THE STOCK

A building lift is a vehicle, not unlike a very short vertical railway. And like a railway, there are two parts to the system: the shaft in which the lift travels up and down; and the 'rolling stock', which in this case means the big motor that pulls the lift cables. The actual box that we all travel in is a fairly inconsequential and inexpensive bit of the whole system. The interesting thing about lifts is that the building owner will usually get the rolling stock for much less than the cost of manufacturing it and installing it into the building's lift shaft.

A CAPTIVE MARKET

Why? Well, the lift manufacturer knows that, once the lift is in the shaft, they have something close to a captive market. You can't change lifts like you might change your car if you fancy a newer model. Your building (if it's more than a couple of storeys high) is entirely unusable without the lift, and the lift has to be maintained rigorously in order to comply with building standards (and to avoid the risk of sending your tenants to a screaming death, something that the more ethical commercial landlord also cares about). All of these considerations would suggest that a lot of negotiating power would gravitate towards the lift-maintenance guys, and that lift-maintenance contracts would tend to be very attractively priced – for the lift-maintenance guys, that is.

A CONTRACT KILLING

And that is indeed the case. In a lot of cases, it's worth it to install a lift system for well below cost, in order to get hold of the lucrative multi-year lift-maintenance contract. And once the lift and its contract is in place, it will go on paying out for years and years and years. Furthermore, the massive cash flow from their installed base of lifts makes it very difficult for anyone to compete against the incumbent players in the lift industry – any plucky little 'start-up' lift company would have to offer the same upfront terms to builders, which would be very difficult to finance without the cash flow from an existing portfolio of lifts. Perhaps this won't always be the case and somewhere in Silicon Valley right now is a jeans-wearing entrepreneur who will 'disrupt' the lift industry, but, if that is to happen, someone will need to quite literally think outside the box. Because 'the box' looks very much like an oligopoly; nearly all lifts in the world are manufactured by either Otis (USA), Thyssen (Germany), Kone (Finland) and then of course there's Schindler's lifts (Switzerland).

A sharp business brain might think, though – couldn't you start up a specialist lift-maintenance company, and go around poaching all those lovely lift-maintenance contracts, leaving the unattractive heavy work of manufacturing and installation to the incumbents (who would presumably go bust, since this bit doesn't cover its costs)? Nice idea but…

THE MONOPOLY OF THE BIG FOUR

If you're maintaining an Otis lift, where do you go to get spare parts? Otis. And since the lift of a multi-storey office building is a very large insurance risk indeed, how are you going to convince building owners (and their insurers) that you're reliable? In general, by getting certification of your staff's expertise and training by Otis. You can see how well set up the big manufacturers are to defend their market share. It is just about possible to compete with these guys – there are some independent installation and maintenance companies, but they're not usually as profitable as the big integrated manufacturers, and the Big Four have something close to a monopoly (or, in the view of the European Competition Commission in

2007, an actual monopoly) on the really big contracts in skyscraper buildings.

LIFT TODAY, PAY TOMORROW

So why do the owners of the buildings agree to these long-dated, usually expensive contracts? Basically, it's swapping an upfront cost now (when the building is being constructed) for a stream of payments later (after the tenants have moved in and started paying rent). Effectively, the lift companies are providing financing, in the form of a cheap lift, and are able to pick up a premium in exchange for structuring their charges to be more convenient for the developer. Of course, the building owner could negotiate harder and get price reductions when the lift-maintenance contract comes up for renewal, but somehow it always seems to be the case that, around that time, an important part of the lift mechanism itself is also scheduled for replacement, which would be a very expensive lump sum payment to make ... unless you sign up for another contract...

COMEDY OF ERRORS

So, let's return to our piano-removal operation. The piano in question is being jingled and jangled about by Laurel and Hardy, and it is clear that the business dynamics in operation are very different. Your removal company certainly has no service contract following the piano later, there are no joint removal and piano-tuning companies in operation. Indeed, the removal company can have only a very slight expectation of ever getting any repeat business from you at all. Therefore, they have to load all of their costs upfront, at the point of delivery. They have to charge you what it actually costs to move a large heavy item from one location, round corners, up stairs, to another. And because this is a time-consuming and people-heavy (literally) operation, it's not cheap. Which is why the piano owner turned to Laurel and Hardy in the first place, because they were.

The owner of the house learned of his mistake, though, when the donkey, providing the counter-balance for the piano of course, crashed in through their first-floor window. And the piano smashed on the ground just for good measure. All in all, better leave it to the professionals and pay the real price, too.

WHY ARE TRADE SHOWS THE PERFECT BUSINESSES?

Essentially, what trade shows achieve is the magic bullet of business. If you are lucky enough to run a company that organises trade shows, the deal you are pulling off is this: getting people to pay you for the privilege of showing off their goods, then getting other people to pay you for the privilege of looking at them. Not many industries can get the kind of enviable economics when you're taking money from both sides of the house – to be honest, it's pretty much only Peter Stringfellow and trade shows. The economics of the latter are actually a lot more interesting; diving into the business models of strip clubs basically only turns up a lot of faintly depressing cases about what constitutes the dividing line between an 'employee' and an 'independent contractor' for the purposes of tax, employers' NI, unfair dismissal tribunals, etc. But trade shows – get a good one and you've got an earner for life.

Seriously, if any readers are aware of a medium-sized industry, profession or market that doesn't have a single big, dominant trade show, get in touch with us. We know people who can make it happen, and we can cut a deal on the back-end royalties. The right to organise a specific successful trade show is a valuable thing, and they are occasionally bought and sold, like newspaper mastheads.

HEADS WE WIN, TAILS WE WIN

But what are the pitfalls? Well, as our facetious analogy shows, the operator of the trade show gets his or her position by providing the focal point where a lot of people who basically already want to meet each other can do so, in a convenient location. It's useful to the customers to be able to see a lot of producers all at once, rather than having to traipse round either physically or virtually. And the producers want to show up because there will be customers there – a trade-show booth is a cost-efficient form of advertising, particularly for larger-ticket items, because it generates a manageable number of specific, pre-qualified sales leads.

And also, for the right kind of person, trade shows can be fun – they're a chance to have a day out of the office and catch up with mates in the same industry for a gossip and an expense-account boozy lunch. Part of the skill of trade show events management is knowing what balance to strike between serious speaker sessions and more celebrity-oriented or entertaining ones; you need to know how much of a good time your interest group likes to have, and how much of a jolly the bosses are prepared to pay for. And this factor has considerable cyclical variation – the commodities and financial services industry trade shows can range from being three day spectaculars in Rome in a boom year, to an afternoon in the ExCeL Centre following a bust.

THE IN-CROWD

The thing is, it's a chicken and egg situation. The customers only want to show up if there are enough producers there to make it worth their while, but the producers only want to show up if there are enough customers there to make it worth their while. There are few things sadder than the fourth- or fifth-most prestigious trade show in an industry in a bad year as you watch half a dozen junior executives without cheque-writing authority amble past a row of unsold booth space. Since the providers of conference halls (and the ancillary services of sound, lighting and even catering) are aware of the amount of money that a trade show has knocking around, they tend to charge wedding-party rates, and a badly thought-out trade show that has to be cancelled for lack of interest can be a financial disaster.

THE 'MATTHEW EFFECT'

For to the one who has, more shall be given ... but from he who has not, even what he has shall be taken away (Matthew 13:12)

So you need to get your trade show right, particularly if you are starting up a new show to compete with established incumbents. But even the biggest shows can fail if they don't generate enough of the right sort of footfall as Australia's official fashion week trade show, Premiere, found out in April 2013. Exhibitors left in disgust, having not taken any orders, blaming the relocation of the trade show element away from the real fun of the event, the model runway shows. And the provision of fun, sun, booze and after-dinner speeches from semi-established standup comedy stars can only get you so far. The big attractions that get a trade show going are the keynote speakers. Again, the strange economics of the industry come into play. For top-quality speakers, you might have to pay decent money. But some of the very best attractions are people who usually don't cost anything at all – they're industry players who are important because they might make (or even better, might promise to make, in time for you to get the marketing material printed) a big announcement or product launch on the stage at your trade show. That is the apotheosis of the industry – top-quality monetisable content, for free – but, obviously, people are only going to do that for the very best trade shows. Which gives the incumbent top shows a massive competitive advantage over any upstarts.

This is another example of the Matthew Effect (named after the gospel of Matthew) – whereby initial advantage creates further advantage, and can be summarised as 'The rich get richer and the poor get poorer'. Can you see why a really dominant trade show is such a valuable property?

FIRST MOVER ADVANTAGE
And there is obviously very big first mover advantage in this industry. The easiest way to be the biggest trade show is to be the *only* trade show. And, in turn, the easiest way to be the only trade show is to be the first trade show in a new industry. New industries grow up

all the time, and surprisingly often their key players are too busy disrupting the norm, or creating the new world, to realise that what they need is a really good old slap-up trade show. Spotting the moment when a new industry is big enough to sustain a trade show is a real driver of success in the industry, and it's a talent that some people have, not unlike Simon Cowell's instinct for a boy band.

STELLAR POWER

One of the most productive sources of new industries, of course, is old industries and so one of the best places to look for the material of new trade shows is the most exciting booth areas of existing trade shows. Knowing when to bud off a new trade show from an old one is a key skill in this industry – the firm that realised that 'solar power' was now a big enough component of 'renewable energy' did as well as the guys that realised that 'renewable energy' was a big enough component of the electricity generation industry to warrant its own trade show. Once more, this is a skill that anyone familiar with the music industry will recognise – a trade show has got to be big enough to support a critical mass of paying punters, but not so big that it's got two or three trade competitors already.

So, to anyone with an idea for a trade show, our offer stands. Seriously. Fifty-fifty split if it comes off.

SHE SHORT-SELLS SHOES ON A SHORT-SALES SHOE SITE

OR, HOW VOLKSWAGEN BANKRUPTED THE HEDGE FUNDS

A lot of people seem to struggle to understand how people make money in the stock market by 'betting on shares to go down'. Actually, you can do this yourself, and you don't even have to have a brokerage account to do it. All you need is eBay, and an opinion on the likely future direction of the price of something. Say, you've just developed an opinion (shared by at least one of the authors) that Jimmy Choo women's shoes are wildly overpriced...

'SCUSE, CAN I 'BORROW' YOUR SHOES?
Step one, you 'borrow' a pair of these overpriced shoes from your sister/best friend/more highly paid colleague.

Then sell them on eBay for the current average price, and pocket the cash. Put it safely away, i.e. in a shoebox. When the irate female you borrowed them from starts asking for her Jimmy Choos back, go out and buy a pair at your local second-hand designer shoe shop, using the cash that you've kept in your special shoebox shoe trading account. If your prediction is right, and the price has gone down, then you will have some money left over in the shoebox, after 'closing out' the transaction, and this is your profit.

BACK OF THE SHOEBOX

On the other hand, maybe you don't want to close out your trade just because a certain femme fatale wants her shoes back – perhaps the price hasn't moved in your direction as far or as fast as you wanted it to (or indeed at all). In this case, you can keep the trade open by finding another long-suffering woman with a pair of Jimmy Choo shoes that she doesn't want to wear that evening, and deliver those to your first victim instead, keeping yourself in the position of having one pair of borrowed shoes (and thus an obligation to return a pair of Jimmy Choo shoes at some date in the future – this is your 'short position'), and one sum of eBay sale proceeds in cash in your shoebox.

SHORT POSITION

Effectively, 'betting' that the price of a share will go down. The way this is achieved is to borrow the share and sell it, in the hope that, when you have to return the share, you will be able to buy it back in the market for a lower price.

Sharper readers will be objecting at this point that this sounds pretty unrealistic. (Not the bit where there are loads of women with vast collections of unworn shoes in their cupboards, that's spot on.) But the bit where you can find exactly the specification of shoes that you borrowed in order to return a pair to the first shoe-deprived lady that she will recognise as equivalent to the ones that you borrowed.

HOW DARE YOU SAY MY SHOES ARE FUNGIBLE?

This is a real problem with the analogy – although all equity shares in any given business are pretty much identical, shoes aren't. If I have a share in BT or IBM, it's exactly the same in form and function as a share you own in the same company. This is why loads of people short-sell shares, but many fewer try to short-sell shoes. What we are talking about here is called 'fungibility' – the property of being able to deliver one asset in place of another. In general, all of a company's shares will be fungible for each other in exactly the way that shoes aren't. There is no reason whatsoever that someone would be able to tell the difference between two different shares, as the only difference that exists is the serial number and the record of who owns it. Of course, some people would argue the same is true with shoes, but they are ignorant and wrong. (Readers may sense that the authors are not speaking wholly with one voice in this chapter.)

FUNGIBILITY

A piece of financial jargon effectively meaning that two bits of paper are interchangeable. Pound notes are fungible – it doesn't matter which particular one you have. So are most shares. Bonds, however, are not necessarily fungible – different bonds have different maturities and interest payments. In the world of physical objects, hammers and shovels are pretty fungible – wedding rings, decidedly less so.

BONDAGE

However, the situation with bonds is different. If a company has bonds outstanding, then you can't rely on the bonds to be sufficiently identical to be fungible. Typically, a company will have different bonds with different coupons and maturities, and you can't deliver one of the ten-year bonds if you borrowed one of the five-year bonds. Since the bonds are issued in large unit sizes, and bonds are generally fungible within each issue (as long as the coupon and maturity are the same, by and large), this doesn't mean that it's impossible to short-sell bonds. But it is a lot more difficult, even if you have the assistance of a really good broker.

BONDS

A bond is a tradeable loan issued by a company or a government. Company bonds are a way of raising money for a company – rather than borrowing money from the bank, the company sells IOUs to the public.

SWAPPING CREDIT

That, in summary, is a large part of the reason why the credit default swap (CDS) was invented. It had always been irksome to that part of the bond market that spends its time analysing the creditworthiness of companies that there was no easy way to trade based on the predictions their analysis threw up. If you wanted to sell a company's credit risk because you thought it was risky, you would have to short-sell a specific bond. And bonds are in general more difficult to borrow than shares; the owners have this irritating habit of wanting their bond back when they need to realise some coupon or principal income, leaving you scrambling around for a replacement. With the CDS, however, the trading is concentrated in one (imaginary) security and, because it's a derivatives contract, there is no question of needing to borrow or deliver the underlying securities – you just make bets with other investors and settle up periodically based on the price where the bonds trade.

CREDIT DEFAULT SWAP

This is a derivatives contract that pays out a sum of money if a particular company defaults on its debt.

THE NAKED SHORT SALE

One more thing to let you know about – and we don't advise doing this – but, if you're feeling particularly lairy, then there is a way to sell shoes short with a bit less effort, but a lot more risk, and it is even almost legal in some but not all jurisdictions. Say, you want to short-sell the even more overpriced Christian Louboutins, but your sister only has Jimmy Choos (and the two aren't fungible, believe me). You could copy a picture of some Louboutins off the web, and put up an auction on eBay with thirty days' delivery, trusting in your own ability to scrounge some up from somewhere at a lower price within the next month.

Now this is very much against the terms and conditions of eBay and, if you are caught doing this sort of thing a lot, your account will probably be suspended. The reason is pretty clear of course – eBay know that auctions of this sort tend to result in failed deliveries and unsatisfied customers pretty frequently, and they also know that this kind of failure tends to reflect on people's perceptions of eBay as a whole.

When traders do the equivalent thing on a stock market – selling a stock short without first finding the borrow – it's called a 'naked short sale'. This is almost as exciting as it sounds, and so it's illegal in a lot of markets.

AND HOW VOLKSWAGEN BECAME THE MOST VALUABLE CAR COMPANY ON EARTH, VERY BRIEFLY

Even when it's not illegal, it's really very risky. The danger with naked short-selling is that, without the constraint of needing to borrow shares before shorting them, it is possible for there to be more short positions than there are shares available. When this happens, it's not even mathematically possible for all the short-sellers to deliver all their shares and, in the resulting 'squeeze', some pretty alarming things can happen. This isn't just a theoretical possibility: it happens in real life in markets where naked short sales aren't banned. In 2007, a bunch of hedge funds badly underestimated the proportion of Volkswagen shares that were controlled by the Porsche corporate treasury. When they got the bad news and all scrambled to try to get hold of the small number of shares available, the price went up so far that Volkswagen briefly became the most valuable car company in the world, by market capitalisation.

A few hedge funds disappeared forever due to the losses on that one, because, while the most you can lose by buying a share is all your money, the losses on a short sale are theoretically unlimited.

As the proverb goes:
'He who sells what isn't his'n
Must buy it back, or go to prison.'

Or as another proverb goes:
'Get away from my shoes!'

MINSKY MOMENTS

If you're ever asked to provide forecasts for the overall economic environment – well, in fact, should this ever happen, then what we'd truly advise is to find some way of sliding out of the responsibility as it's a thankless task even for people who are paid to do it – the best thing to do is to find the website of a central bank or similar, take their forecasts as a bill of goods, and then trust that nobody will ever either check up on how well the macro bit of the projections turned out, or really blame you all that much if the answer is 'terrible'.

On the other hand, if you find yourself in the position of *actually needing*, for your own purposes, to have a general idea of how the economy might turn out, or to be able to say something sensible about the risk of an otherwise decent idea being blindsided by a global calamity, then ... nothing's certain, but we've had reasonable results in the past in making crash predictions based on a back-of-the-envelope assessment about how 'fragile' the typical financial structure has got to be, in order to suggest that we're all going to hell in a handcart.

FINANCIAL INSTABILITY

If you read the financial papers, you'll occasionally see the phrase 'Minsky moment' used to describe, usually with extensive benefit of hindsight, the tipping point at which some economic structure or other took its first steps on the road that led to hell. If you read the excellent book *Manias, Panics and Crashes* by Charles Kindleberger, you'll come across a summary of the ideas of the 1950s economist Hyman Minsky. If you've read *Financial Instability* by Minsky or any of his academic papers, then, to be honest, we're a bit scared of you – they're hard to find, pretty technical and not always very clearly written. It is fair to say that Minsky is a lot more admired than read and a lot more cited than understood, and that in general a very high percentage of the people who ever use the phrase 'Minsky moment' have only heard of Minsky via Kindleberger, if that.

What we're saying here is that you shouldn't feel bad

for chucking his name about based only on the summary we're about to give. That's not to say you shouldn't bother with the Kindleberger book – it's a classic of the financial literature and a great aeroplane read too. But our summary is much shorter.

THE CYCLE

So, here goes. Minsky's financial instability hypothesis, in a nutshell: good times cause people to take on debt – to use the jargon, they 'increase their leverage', but this just means that they do more things financed with borrowed money, and less with their own individual or corporate savings. Leverage leads to risk. Risk leads to bad times. As a theory of the business cycle, there are a lot of technical criticisms to be made, but it's got a good intuitive feel to it and it matches up to the really big disasters pretty well.

LEVERAGE
The amount of debt that a company (or some other project) has. The analogy is to mechanical leverage because it increases the profits if things go right (you only have to pay back the debt, you don't have to share the upside), but increases the losses if they don't (you still have to pay back the debt if you don't make any profits at all).

THE SECRET LIFE OF MONEY

WHICH PART OF THE CYCLE ARE YOU IN?

But in this form it's hardly a guide to action. Luckily, Minsky gave some pointers about how to identify what phase of the cycle you're in. What you need to do is look for the typical financial structure around you, and decide which category it fits into. Minsky gives you a choice of three.

Hedge: 'Hedged' financial structures are cash flow positive. The money that's coming in is enough to cover the interest payments on the debt, and to pay back the principal of the debt in a reasonable amount of time. By definition, these hedged financial structures are cautious, non-risk-taking structures. Think of a twenty-five-year mortgage to a civil servant, for three times their salary. Or a loan to finance a retailer's purchase of goods overseas, where the sale of the goods will generate enough cash to repay the loan.

Speculative: Speculative financial structures are still cash flow positive, but are only paying down the debt very slowly. If something is dependent on being able to 'roll over' its debt (i.e. to take out a new loan when the old one falls due), then it's speculative. Think of a manufacturing company that is taking out a five-year bank loan to install machine tools that will last twenty years. At the end of the five years, the bank gets to make the decision whether to roll over the loan (which it will do if the company is servicing its debt well and making a profit), or to foreclose (which it will do if the company is not making money and it needs to sell the assets to get the loan paid back).

Ponzi: A 'Ponzi' investment is named after Charles Ponzi, a famous conman who promised vast returns to investors, which he delivered for a while, by paying out returns not from profits of the investments, but purely from new capital brought in by new investors. Such schemes are a staple of con artists, as seen, for example, with the recent scandal of Bernie Madoff who made off with people's money in exactly the same way. In Minsky's terminology, a Ponzi investment is one that isn't even covering its interest payments – not only does the debt have to be rolled over, but also each successive rollover is bigger than the one before (because it needs to refinance the rolled-up interest payments). Think of a dot com start-up, which is going to need several rounds of financing before it even starts turning a profit.

You can tell from the names of the categories that some of them are somewhat more pejorative than others – being in a Ponzi category certainly doesn't sound ideal.

In actual fact, the last two categories shouldn't be

regarded as intrinsically or invariably bad. Nearly all property development, for example, has (at best) a speculative structure, because it has a long time horizon before it turns profitable, significantly longer than the maximum term that anyone is prepared to lend to property developers. Banks prefer to keep the term of their lending short, because it increases their control – at every loan rollover, they can either keep the project going, or shut it down and sell the assets half-made.

What we're saying here is don't get hung up on the terminology – 'Ponzi' and 'speculative' don't necessarily mean 'bad'. An awful lot of the most important things in the modern world started off – or were at some point in their lives – financed on a Ponzi basis. After all, if you went to university and took out student loans, the chances are that your university education had a Ponzi financial structure – for all the time you were at college, you were increasing your debt rather than servicing it, in the assumption that at some point in the future you'd start generating cash flows to pay it back.

SPOTTING THE BUBBLE

While individual speculative or Ponzi schemes aren't necessarily bad, the problems start when these more fragile structures start to become dominant in the economy, or when economic units that don't realistically have the kind of explosive growth prospects that might justify something other than a hedge structure start getting into speculative (let alone Ponzi) territory. So, if you see big leveraged buyouts of very mature companies, you should start getting nervous. Or property companies with a portfolio of third-tier shopping centres in provincial towns being financed as if they were building office blocks in Mayfair.

Or (and this is how one of the authors spotted, in writing and six months ahead of the event, the bursting of the Irish property bubble), you can sometimes see structures that were towards the more adventurous end of hedge financing getting pushed, en masse, into speculative or Ponzi territory by either a structural rise in their interest bill, or a structural fall in their earnings. It's usually not hard to get a back-of-the-envelope calculation of the average cash flow of a business, and it's usually not too hard to get a back-of-the-envelope estimate of the fixed costs (debt service and rent) that this cash flow has got to cover. When you see a big shift in the ratio between the two, then you know you're looking at a fragile situation.

If you're looking to go crisis-spotting, that's the best way to go about it, in our opinion. Some readers might feel a bit short-changed here – all we've done is give a few pointers and aphorisms about things to watch out for, not a step–by-step guide to making macroeconomic predictions. But really – did you think there was an *easy* way to do this stuff?

THE MALT WHISKY
YIELD CURVE

How do you make a barrel of twelve-year-old whisky? Start with a barrel of eleven-year-old whisky and wait. That's not even really a joke; it's a fairly fundamental fact about the production of brown spirits. For most types of consumer goods, you can increase and decrease production more or less at will, but, with a product where long aging (either in barrels like whisky, or in bottles like wine) is an intrinsic part of the process, your maximum output this year is determined by how much of the stuff you laid down in the past.

HOW INTERESTING...
This also means that, because the passage of time is a

vital input to the process, the rate of interest is important to the production of Scotch whisky in a much more direct way than to most other goods. The amount of time between paying the cost (including the labour cost) of making the product, and getting the cash in from selling it, is important in all sorts of industries, from management consulting to Airbus manufacture. However, in the brown spirits trade, it's much easier to identify the specific amount of interest that is attributable to a particular batch of product, which is why for a very long time, whisky makers were one of the very few industries that were allowed to hold 'capitalised interest cost' on their balance sheets. This meant that they could treat some of their past interest as part of the cost of the asset they'd bought (the barrel of whisky) rather than past expenses, which were gone forever.

In an ideal world, of course, this wouldn't make a difference, as everybody would concentrate only on cash flowing in and out, plus changes in the market value of investments. In the real world, however, it makes a big difference to the way the accounts are recorded; if you didn't include the interest expense of waiting around for whisky to mature, distilleries would look like weird, inefficient companies that borrowed loads of money for no reason at all, and were constantly rescued from their stupid financing decisions by unexpected capital gains on selling vats of spirits that cost them next to nothing to make.

WHISKY IN THE JAR

Given that a substantial part of the cost of making whisky is the cost of waiting for it to mature, how does this affect the value of the whisky in the barrel? Or to put it another way, what happens to a barrel of nine-year-old whisky as it turns into a barrel of ten-year-old whisky? If we calculate the percentage difference in price from one year to the next, what does that match up to in the real world?

THE ANGEL TAKES THE TOPMOST

Well, the first thing that happens is that the ten-year-old barrel has slightly less whisky in it than the nine-year-old barrel did, because of evaporation (called the 'angels' share' by the marketing departments of whisky distilleries; we suspect, but can't prove, that the people who actually make the stuff might have a more prosaic term). So the distiller would hope to be compensated for this by an increase in the value of the stuff that's left, otherwise they wouldn't leave it in the barrel. So, when we're thinking about the 'malt whisky rate of interest',

THE SECRET LIFE OF MONEY

presume that we're talking about the pure cost of waiting, with an allowance built in for this kind of loss. This is a quite common way to think about industries where part of your return is capitalised interest but where waiting around incurs some costs, like allowing for the bad debt losses on a loan book, or the cost of insurance and storage of a warehouse full of platinum ingots.

MONEY IN THE BANK?

And the previous paragraph might have given you a clue as to how to think about the rate of return on whisky in the barrel. Given that the owner of the barrel has the option to open it and bottle the whisky at any point (after the first five years – spirit younger than that can't be sold as Scotch whisky at all), they therefore have to expect the value of whisky in the barrel to rise by at least the same percentage amount as the interest rate on money in the bank. Otherwise, nobody would hold ten-year-old whisky barrels – it would be more profitable to bottle and sell the nine-year-old whisky and put the money in the bank for the tenth year, and so on right back until it is only five years old and becomes eligible to be called whisky at all.

And similarly, you wouldn't expect whisky in the barrel to rise by much more than the rate of interest, because otherwise everyone would want to own barrels of whisky rather than putting their money in the banks. And so, we would expect to see that the 'malt whisky yield curve' – the difference between a six-year-old and a seven-year old bottle, between a nine-year-old and a ten-year-old, and so forth and so on – would, in principle, be a flat line; the difference between prices of different ages of whisky would be just enough to make a marginal producer indifferent between bottling the whisky now, versus leaving it in the barrel (and incurring storage costs and angels' share) for another year.

FINANCIAL THEORY INTO BUSINESS PRACTICE

Incredibly, this is a piece of financial theory that works! If you were to download the prices of malts from the Scotch Whisky Society website (the whiskies for sale there often come from some quite famous distilleries, but are anonymised, so we don't have to worry so much about branding concerns), you would get a pretty messy scatterplot. If you draw a line of best fit, it gives you an average relationship between price and time that is equivalent to a 4.5 per cent implied annual appreciation rate for Scotch whisky in the barrel. Which compares to an interest rate on money in the bank of 1 per cent, leaving 3.5 per cent for angels' share and storage. This is the kind of relationship that we would call 'order of magnitude correct'. Another way of putting this would be 'wrong, but not so terribly wrong as to invalidate the original idea'.

SENSIBLE SHOES

Why is the relationship so close to that predicted by economic theory when usually economic theory and actual business practice are poles apart? There are several possible answers to this question, but the one that seems most likely to us is the simplest – most distillery managers have been to business school and are fully aware of the principles we've outlined above. People go on a lot about the invisible hand of the market, but actually these days you don't get put in charge of many important things without, at the very least, a sensible accountant holding the ropes. It's often a good tip when you're on a consultancy assignment; look for a studious sensible-shoed ACCA. If they are there, then you can usually be confident that the financial basics have been looked after and concentrate on the big picture issues of customer demand, market identification and so on. If they're not, then it's worth casting an eye over the pricing policy, capital expenditure policies, etc., because there might be some big and easy wins – improving the bottom line by paying attention to things like interest expense.

IF PAYDAY LENDERS' INTEREST RATES ARE SO HIGH, WHY DON'T THEY OWN THE ENTIRE WORLD?

Payday lenders are big business, and they are also mighty controversial. They have come in many guises through the years, from door-to-door loan sharks, with or without accompanying heavies, to modern day Wonga.com and others, and they have all attracted very negative publicity, even while their businesses grow and grow. The negative publicity is often centred around cases of clear financial mis-practice, which we will not go into here, but the publicity is also focused on something we would like to discuss, their very high rates of borrowing – their APR – sometimes quoted as being as high as 6000 per cent.

THE MAN WHO OWNS THE WORLD?

While it is true that the modern-day payday lenders are finding booming business, especially in the UK, at compound interest rates of over 1000 per cent APR, you would expect them to be an even more prominent force than they are. Take a look at the numbers:

Let's take a comparatively modest APR of 780 per cent. If you invest £1,000 at 780 per cent compound interest rate, then in five years it will have grown to £52m, yes, that's £52 million. In eight and a quarter years it will have become £62 trillion ($100 trillion, at the time of writing), which is a bit more than the total GDP of the entire world. After ten years you would have £2.75 quadrillion, which is enough to buy the world five times over.

Although Wonga.com is big, and has ambitions to grow, it is clearly not the case that it, and similar businesses, are growing to the extent that they will soon own the entire world. So what is going on?

IT ALL ADDS UP

You might expect the answer to have to do with loan defaults, but, although they do happen, this is not the core reason. The answer instead is to do with the mathematics of compounding. Say I lend you £30 until payday in ten days' time, and my administrative costs of doing this are £1.71 (i.e. twenty minutes' time for a clerk on minimum wage). If I'm going to cover my costs, then that's a 5.7 per cent charge per ten-day loan. To convert this to an annual percentage rate, take $1.057^{(365/10)}-1$, which is 656 per cent! But of course, I don't get an annual compound of 656 per cent, because I only have your money for ten days.

This is why we don't believe that it makes sense to think about payday loans in terms of APRs.

THE REAL COST OF SHORT-TERM BORROWING

What's at work here is that, if there is any element of fixed costs, which, by definition there must be, then it is very inefficient indeed to borrow small amounts of money for short periods of time. Sure, it would be cheaper for customers of payday lenders to borrow at credit card rates of 17.9 per cent APR, or even bank loan or mortgage rates of substantially less, but this is just saying that it would be cheaper for them to have access to the sorts of financial instruments that are generally not available to customers of payday lenders.

So our conclusion is that, instead of jumping up and down about fictional APRs, the regulating authorities might more usefully facilitate wider societal access to the benefits of low-priced controlled debt.

WHO ARE RIP-OFF LABEL JEANS ACTUALLY RIPPING OFF?

Designers of the high-end label jeans, clothes, bags, etc. that we apparently love to buy make their income from designing. This means that, if someone, most likely someone in Asia, copies their design and then we buy this product instead, we are depriving the designer of their rightful income, right? This is the standard tale told by the 'don't buy fake jeans' brigade; and clampdowns on such fakery are regularly publicised in the media.

THE DESIGNER WEARS PRADA
But if we unpick this story a little more, we see some hidden complexities. The designers of the product that is being copied have already garnered their income

from their design because the design has already been sold at the original high price. That is how it became a high-prestige product that became a target for copying. However, the designer's income from the product's design is usually hard to precisely pin down because the designer is usually a paid employee of a company, such as Prada or Gucci, and the (often monster) profits flow not to the designer, but to the company owners or partners.

WORKING FOR DA BOSS

These owners may be the original founders of the business, they may be members of the public if it is a traded company, they may be pension funds and life assurance companies, or they may be the designers themselves. The larger the company, and the larger the global impact of the brand, the less likely it is that the designers own any significant part of the company.

Therefore, where the designer is a paid employee drawing a salary from the company – which may be supplemented by bonuses in cases of the company achieving financial success – the designer has already been paid for their design. The excess profits generated from a design catching a mood and becoming a copied trend were never due to flow to the designer, but to the owners of the company.

BREAKING DOWN THE FOODCHAIN

For any mass consumer product, whether jeans, or jumpers, or shoes or headphones, the manufacturing process involves a great number of people in manual labour as well as some individuals sitting pretty, designing in London or New York offices. And so for any mass consumer product, all the people in the foodchain who actually make the product were always paid the same low wage, and very often the wages and conditions in the chain making 'genuine' branded products and those making the 'counterfeit' products are interchangeable.

WHAT MAKES FAKE FAKE?

In what sense are 'counterfeit' jeans counterfeit? They're still jeans. Does the fact that they are not made by the official branded factory make a difference to their actual quality as jeans? Industry experts would argue that there certainly is a difference, and personal experience would suggest that there may be a difference, but not such a difference as is reflected in the price differential. £20 'counterfeit' jeans may be a little less well made than 'genuine' £150 jeans, but does the quality differential amount to £130? Almost never. What explains the difference then? The excess profits made by the owners of the company when you choose to buy a branded product. The question at the core of the matter is: which jeans are the rip-off? The 'rip-off' jeans or the 'genuine' jeans?

DR DRE

The answer to this of course varies from case to case – if you pay hundreds of pounds for Dr Dre headphones, you are buying both a well-made product and a high-prestige brand. The tricky task is to separate how much each element is worth to you. Are you really that shallow that the logo of a brand name alone is worth the cost of a meal out? Possibly so, many people are (apparently, they call it being fashionable). But if you aren't, then, as with almost any consumer product, you can obtain an equivalent product with almost identical technical specifications and quality of manufacture for substantially less.

DR DREADFUL

What happens to people who *are* that shallow but don't have hundreds of pounds to spend on headphones? That is when the problems start, because these are the types who go out and buy the fake Dr Dre headphones in a dodgy streetmarket. For, unlike our example of £20 'fake' jeans, which still by and large operate reasonably functionally as jeans, the £5 fake Dr Dre headphones are instead not only unlikely to work well as headphones, but also likely to be very poorly made, highly breakable and worth far less than the apparently 'bargain' price of £5. In these cases, it is the customers who are being right royally ripped off by the rip-off headphone manufacturer.

Dr Dre himself, however, and his monster profits remain intact, as everyone with even half a brain can see the 'rip-off' headphones are indeed rip-offs.

MONEY AND HOW TO USE IT
OR, WHY ARE CREDIT CARD COMPANIES HAPPY TO KEEP CUSTOMERS WHO PAY OFF THEIR BALANCE IN FULL EVERY MONTH?

Running a credit card business is usually a highly profitable thing to do, which is why the market is strongly – although you could argue not strongly enough – regulated. There are three reasons why credit card companies are happy to have customers who pay off their balance in full every month.

MONEY FOR JAM

The first is that, even if a customer pays off their balance in full, credit card companies make money with every transaction they make. Every time you buy something with a credit card, the merchant's bank kicks back a small percentage to your credit card's bank. Credit card nerds, for reasons not worth going into, call this the 'interchange fee'. It is meant to cover the cost of providing the billing system, plus a modicum of fraud protection for the banks; however, successive competition inquiries have tended to find that there is a significant element of rapacious profiteering in there too. So, if you buy something for £100 with a credit card, the retailer might receive only £98. For any major transaction, or any large shop, this is regarded as purely a cost of doing business, and the retailers' agreement with the card providers usually makes them promise that they will not lead customers to favour one means of payment over another. But, for a small shop, or a small transaction, it can wipe out a substantial amount of the merchant's profit, which is why small retailers set minimum transactions for credit card use.

MONEY FOR NOTHING

The second reason is that some credit cards charge an annual fee to customers for the privilege of access to their profit-making spending. We have only one thing to say about this: it is the very rare customer who derives value from the additional benefit of a credit card with an annual fee. In the majority of cases, the benefits offered by the credit card companies are not taken up, and they keep the change.

JAM TODAY, JAM TOMORROW

The third reason why credit card companies are happy to have some customers who pay off their balance in full is because most people don't. Research has found that almost half of all people with credit cards in the UK don't pay off their balance in full, and on average take ten months before the borrowing is paid off. This amounts to interest payments of £2.3bn each year, which are paid to the nation's credit card companies. With this amount of extra cash floating around their system, the credit card companies can well afford to offer credit card facilities for free to people who *do* pay off their balance every month. And of course, they can keep hoping on the off chance that you might slip up: make a late payment, or spend over your limit, or even change your mind, and stop paying off in full every month, and then they are in clover...

WHEN DEBT IS GOOD

Most of us will develop an intimate relationship with debt for much of our lives, whether through our mortgages or credit cards or both. It is not too strong to say that access to debt is a vital part of a growing developed economy, and that one of the most common features of underdeveloped countries is poor access by many of the country's citizens to debt. To misquote Gordon Gekko, debt can be good. Debt can work. But it can also be a helluva nightmare if you don't get it right.

THE GIRL WITH THE CURL

Credit cards are like the girl with the curl in the middle of her forehead – when they are good they are very, very good, but when they are bad they are horrid. Credit cards are very good at three things:

1. Credit cards provide short-term debt for free, which allows spending next month's salary today. By using balance transfers cleverly, credit cards can give you free debt for longer than this, often up to eighteen months.
2. Spending on plastic can generate cash back on every purchase with the right card.
3. Buying with a credit card provides protection over purchases – paying for something that costs over £100 with a credit card (*not* with a debit card) means that by law the credit card company is jointly liable with the

retailer for consumer rights. So, if the company that made the product goes bust, the credit card company is liable for the full cost of the item, and in fact this is true if only a tiny fraction (say, £1) of the item is paid for by credit card.

WHEN CREDIT CARD COMPANIES MAKE STARTLING SUMS

But credit card companies charge notoriously high levels of interest, 19 per cent APR is the average, and these have a huge impact when only the minimum repayment each month is made. Even a small balance will result in paying the credit card company a frightening amount of money by the time the debt is paid off, especially for cards with high APRs, such as store cards. These are often the easiest to apply for, undertaking the fewest credit checks, but have the highest interest rates for repaying the loan.

A DEBTOR'S PRISON

But what about a larger balance, say £3,000, the average credit card balance in the UK over the last few years? The UK has the highest average credit card balance figure in Europe, by the way. Like topping the charts in the teenage pregnancy rate, this is not something to be proud of. A minimum repayment of 2 per cent of an average £3,000 balance would be £60 each month, take over fifty years before the debt was paid off, and cost an extra nearly £10,000 in interest payments to the credit card company. Many store cards require only minimum payments of 1 per cent of the debt per month; at this rate the debt would hang around for ever, as the minimum payment is insufficient to repay the capital plus interest.

NO SYMPATHY FOR THE DEVIL

This is why on credit card application forms the 'minimum repayment' box is often pre-ticked by the company, because this is how they make money hand over fist. Of course, when debt lasts this long, it is possible that at some point the debtor will default on the debt and the credit card company will have to live with non-repayment. But the initial amount they loaned will generally have been repaid several times over by then.

CASH ADVANCES ARE EVEN MORE PROFITABLE

And if credit card companies manage to persuade people to take out cash advances against their card, the rates they charge are even higher. Fees of 3 per cent of the cash withdrawn are typical, then this amount is added to the withdrawn amount and the whole lot is added to the credit card balance. Then, to add insult to injury, an even higher interest fee than usual is generally charged on the balance that comes from the cash withdrawal.

HIDDEN FEES

Lastly, credit card companies also have a further notorious way of driving up their profits, by the use of hidden fees. A fee of £25 for a late payment of a monthly bill is typical. Companies even charge fees of £25 or £30 for spending over the set limit.

With all of these many and varied ways of deriving profits from a piece of plastic, it's no wonder credit card companies are happy to provide monthly credit to customers who pay off their balance in full every month. Just make sure you're one of them.

CRAB-FISHING DEATHS AND AMERICAN PRESIDENTS

OR, WHY IT MIGHT MAKE SENSE TO GIVE 110 PER CENT EFFORT, BUT ONLY FOR A WHILE

What's the most dangerous job in America? We're talking about the normal measure for occupational hazard – the number of job-related deaths per 100,000 worker-years. Have a guess...

The most dangerous job in America, by that metric, is President of the USA. Really. There have been 225 worker-years for that job since 1789 (225 years multiplied by a workforce of 1, obviously). During that period, there have been four assassinations – Lincoln, Garfield, McKinley and Kennedy. Being assassinated surely has to be the definition of a job-related fatality. Plus add to that the death of William Henry Harrison, from pneumonia caught as a result of standing around waiting for his inauguration in the cold (yes, genuinely, we're not making this up), which has to count in health and safety terms as a failure of the employer's duty to provide safe working conditions. Doing the maths, that's one death every 45 worker-years (225/5=45), or a rate of 2,222 fatalities per 100,000 worker-years. That's insanely dangerous; just under an eighth of all the people who have ever done this job have been killed by it! Even if you consider this to be a bit of a cheat and want to start the clock with the moment when the Secret Service were given the job of protecting the President (in 1902), the Kennedy assassination means that the job-related death rate has been 892 per 100kW/y.

LINCOLN, KENNEDY, CRAB FISHERS...

All of which makes two points: being President of America is potentially risky for your health, but more importantly, if you extrapolate from small samples, you had better take care in interpreting the results. So to return to the original question – what is the most dangerous job that is actually carried out by enough people to make the statistics valid?

The answer has historically been 'Pacific Northwest Crab Fisherman', with a death rate of around 400 per

100kW/y. Fishing is always one of the most dangerous occupations (along with timber cutting and coal mining), and the particular meteorological and economic conditions of the Alaskan crab fishery meant that it was far and away the most dangerous fleet to fish in.

But, actually, the Pacific crab fleet is nothing like as dangerous as it used to be. Since around 2006, fatalities have been no worse than the average for the fishing industry in general. What has changed is the permit system, which has greatly reduced the incentives for dangerous behaviour, and fatalities have fallen as a result.

THE GREATEST SHARE OF THE FISH PIE

Previously, the Alaskan crab fishery was managed by a short permitted fishing season, with the catch limited in its aggregate size – the season began on a given day, and ended when the volume of crabs landed reached the amount that the authorities felt could be sustainably removed. This meant, of course, that any crabs caught by one fishing boat reduced the possible catch of all the rest. Finders keepers, losers weepers meant that the only way to survive economically was to go hell for leather and try to land as many crabs as possible as quickly as possible, competing against other fishermen to take the greatest possible share of the fixed amount.

INDIVIDUAL QUOTAS, FEWER ACCIDENTS

So, the Pacific crab fleet tended to stay out too long, and to go out in conditions that weren't safe, and to carry bigger cargoes than were safe, and in general cut corners on safety in order to race for the catch. But a few years ago the licence system was changed, and instead each registered boat was given its own individual quota. Because the boats weren't effectively taking crabs from each other, they were able to fish at a sensible pace, and the accident rate fell very sharply. Also, since each captain had much more predictable earnings, they were able to borrow money and improve the quality of the boats. It's an interesting study in how incentives affect behaviour.

GIVING MORE THAN 100 PER CENT

It also helps us to give some kind of practical meaning to the hoariest old management cliché of them all – the idea of 'giving 110 per cent'. All sorts of pedants will be very quick to say that this is mathematically impossible, but it isn't if you mean that '100 per cent' is to be taken, not as the maximum possible effort you can put in, but the maximum effort that it's *sensible* to put in. The Alaskan crab fishermen were putting in maybe 120 per cent of the sensible amount of effort or more, and, as a result of that, they had the highest fatality rates of any job on earth.

RUNNING ON EMPTY

Any machine will be rated for its capacity; the amount of output that it should produce. A lot of the skill of managing a manufacturing production line is to keep the machines working as close to 100 per cent of their rated capacity for as much of the time as possible. But if there's a rush order, you can usually run a machine at more than 100 per cent of its rated capacity – the simplest way to do this is to delay scheduled maintenance. You can also turn up the speed of motors, run furnaces hotter, tolerate a higher defect rate and so on. For most of the Second World War, pretty much the entire manufacturing capacity of the UK was running at 110 per cent of maximum output and more.

MONKEYS MINDING MACHINES

But, of course, delaying maintenance is not really a good idea. A machine that's run at 110 per cent is going to wear out more quickly, break down more frequently and produce more variable quality of output. It's something that has to be done from time to time to meet rush orders, but a factory that's always running at 110 per cent is being mismanaged (wartime situations excluded), just as much as one that's always running with loads of spare capacity. And there's a fairly clear analogy to the management of people.

Sometimes, as a manager, you have to ask a team to give 110 per cent. Some industries, like software development, are notorious for having 'crunch' periods towards the end of the development process, because there's a reverse learning curve effect – it's only when you've got a product that's nearly ready to ship that you start finding all the bugs in it, and when you've got a product that's nearly ready to ship, each bug is trickier to fix because more things might be interacting with it. So, in industries like this, as in a lot of creative fields and in investment banking, 110 per cent effort, for a certain period of time, is often a reasonable thing to ask for.

TIME OUT

But people need maintenance too. And if people try to work at more than 100 per cent of their capacity for protracted periods of time, they too will burn out. So, while we'll defend the concept of 'giving it 110 per cent' as a relatively meaningful piece of management jargon, the kind of person who says that they want their employees to 'always give it 110 per cent' ought to be avoided, just in case they mean what they say.

DEPRECIATION – HOW DO YOU WORK IT OUT, AND WHY WOULD YOU BOTHER?

DEPRECIATION

An item in a company's accounts that allows for the fact that the assets will have lost value over a year simply because they are one year older. A familiar concept to buyers of new sports cars.

Depreciation is a simple concept, so it's surprising that so many people get all caught up and confused by it, and even more surprising that so many otherwise sensible people choose to ignore it entirely. It doesn't help that the accountants make it much, much more complicated than it needs to be, always with the very best of intentions. By which we mean the very sneakiest of intentions.

The issue here is that, in accounts, the depreciation charge is subtracted from reported earnings per share, so, in the past (particularly in the 1980s, the real heyday of 'creative accounting'), playing about with it was a popular method for manipulating earnings. Even today, although most of the really egregious accounting loopholes have been shut down by the International Accounting Standards Board, doing a few back-of-the-envelope calculations on the depreciation amount and whether it's a sensible percentage of the total assets is a good way to start looking for 'red flags' or indications that there might be something else crook about the accounts. But since we're not writing a guide for accounting snoops here, we can afford to be general in our thinking, and consider the question of depreciation in a world where everybody is honest about it.

APPRECIATING LIFE

At heart, a 'depreciation life' is an admirably practical compromise over a difficult and probably insolvable philosophical question. The question is: how much value do your possessions lose every year, just because of the passage of time? In business terms, this translates to the question: how much value do the assets on your balance sheet lose every year, just because they are a year older, and therefore how much should you reduce the value of them for accounting purposes? At first glance, it seems like a straightforward question, which should therefore have a straightforward answer – how much value is lost purely due to the physical wearing out of tools and equipment?

DEPRECIATION LIFE

Usually, the depreciation on an asset is calculated by estimating its useful life, and deducting a proportion of its value every year until it is 'fully depreciated'. The depreciation life is only ever a rough estimate, and companies often choose to use substantially shorter estimates than the real useful life, because this lets them take a bigger charge (which is deductible from profits for tax purposes, even though it's not an item of cash you need to pay).

But, in practice, to gain a precise answer to the question in monetary terms is anything but straightforward.

There are many factors at play here; in addition to assets losing value due to wearing out, there are more thorny issues such as the advance of technological obsolescence, the possibility of repairing worn-out kit rather than replacing it and so on. The heart of the problem is that it's actually very rare to replace a piece of capital equipment with one that's exactly the same – the new one will usually be better, so it's impossible to split up an even moderately complicated company's capital spending into 'new investment' versus 'replacement of worn-out old investment'.

RULE OF THUMB RULES OK

The question of what the 'true' rate of depreciation might be is actually one of the big unsolved ones of economics. But it's a question that next to nobody is working on, because there is a 'rule of thumb' approach that seems to work OK – you estimate how long it will be before you buy a new thing to replace an existing thing, divide the amount you paid for the first thing by that number of years, and then set aside that much from every year's earnings to be the 'depreciation charge'.

HAVE VAN, WILL TRAVEL

So (to take the canonical example from accounting textbooks), if you own a removals business and a van costs you £50,000 and lasts five years, then every year you set a depreciation charge equal to £10,000 per van. If you do that, then in years where you don't buy a new van, your expenses will be somewhat lower than the amount of cash you have coming in, and the reserve thus built up will be just about enough to buy a new van when you will need one.

This, by the way, is a good enough summary of why you should always be a bit sniffy about companies that talk a blue streak about 'EBITDA' (earnings before interest, tax, depreciation and amortisation). EBITDA is a decent measure of the cash being thrown off by the business, which is a useful thing to know in a lot of contexts. But, quite apart from the fact that the taxman and the interest bill are not exactly optional extras, any company that is trying to get you to focus on the cash, ignoring depreciation, needs to have a convincing story about why it doesn't need to be building up a piggy bank to replace worn-out assets. Such stories exist (mainly in people-intensive businesses, where the main depreciating assets are things like software licences), but it's worth asking the question.

IS IT A VEHICLE? IS IT A MACHINE TOOL?

Although the textbook example suggests that depreciation is all about the average time something takes to wear out – e.g. how long it takes a shiny new van to turn into a conked-out wreck – the best way to think about the depreciation life is not just in this way. Instead, you should think of depreciation as the average amount that you have to spend on vans every year, in order to make sure that you don't run out of vans. Just like 'debtor days' isn't really worth thinking of as the average time that your debtors take to pay – it's a measure of the amount of customer debt you're carrying on your balance sheet – so depreciation isn't about when you have to pay for something, but rather how much you have to set aside each year so that you will always be able to pay to renew when you need to.

Whatever your business, the way to pick which depreciation life to account any given asset as is to look at a table like the one below (or one from your favourite accountancy textbook) and decide whether the asset you're looking at is more like a vehicle, a machine tool, a computer or a building.

The advantage of training yourself to think about depreciation in this way is that, once you've got used to thinking of 'the depreciation life of a widget' as being related to 'the amount of money that has to be spent

ASSET TYPE	EXAMPLE	LIFE IN YEARS
Furniture/office equipment	Desk, table, chairs	7
Computer hardware	Computer, printer	10
Telephone equipment		15
Motor vehicles		10
Buses		12
Temporary buildings	Portakabin	25
Buildings		50
Heating, ventilation and air-con systems		40
Roofing		20
Electrical/plumbing		30
Kitchen equipment		15
Heavy construction equipment	Bulldozers	20
Scientific/Medical Radio communication Recreational equipment	Lab equipment, treadmills, etc.	15
Land improvements	Fencing	20
Land		No depreciation
Artwork		No depreciation

on widgets every year, to keep the overall inventory of widgets constant', you will find yourself being able to use depreciation lives for all sorts of purposes.

GOING UP?

Such as forecasting, for example. If you have to estimate the sales of something this year, it's often a good starting point to ask, 'How many of these things are there out there in the world?' and 'What would be a sensible depreciation life?' The first of these is often a relatively easy piece of information to get hold of, and the second can usually reasonably be estimated. Doing the depreciation arithmetic gives you a 'neutral' baseline, and then you can compare the last few years of actual sales to see whether it's lower than the baseline (indicating that widgets may not be replaced as they wear out – a market in terminal decline), or whether it's much higher (indicating that people want to increase the amounts of widgets in their factories). It's most useful when you're forecasting a declining industry (and they need love too; a declining industry is often quite attractive for some kinds of buyer because they don't have much capital expenditure so they throw off quite a lot of cash), because the depreciation rate tells you how fast things are declining.

THE ASSETS THAT WOULD NOT DIE...

And you can also generalise the concept of a depreciation life to think about the depreciation of intangible assets. This is considered a somewhat crook thing to do these days, as it was a source of massive accounting malpractice back in that short period of time when you were allowed to have brands on your balance sheet, and decide on a depreciation charge for them. But it's not a totally invalid concept, and just because it can no longer be declared in annual accounts in this way doesn't mean it's not a helpful tool for thinking about a business. If we remember to think of depreciation not as an 'estimated life' but as 'the amount you need to spend to stop supplies of something from decreasing', then the marketing budget for a brand can be, conceptually at least, split up into 'marketing aimed at increasing sales' and 'marketing aimed at preserving the value of the brand'. The second kind of spending looks very much like something that we would call 'allowance for depreciation' if it was to do with a capital asset.

ASSETS WORTH APPRECIATING

Some capital assets are, quite rightly, not depreciated at all in the accounts, because it is assumed that an amount of money is spent every year on maintaining the existing

73

THE SECRET LIFE OF MONEY

ones instead of making an allowance to buy new ones. Pub companies, most notably for example, don't tend to depreciate their pubs and, as some pubs in England have been around since the thirteenth century without noticeably having worn away to nothing, they've probably got a point.

FOOTFALL CRAZY

In all corners of the retail industry, but particularly in the restaurant trade, people recognise the phenomenon of the 'graveyard site' – a premises that keeps on seeing new businesses open up, trade for a year and then close down again. It isn't usually the result of paranormal activity or because the place is built on the site of a cursed medieval plague pit; it's just the more prosaic fact that the fundamental equation of retailing is:

Sales = footfall x purchases per customer x average ticket

In this equation, 'footfall' means the number of customers who happen to walk past the shop, purchases per customer is what it says, and the 'average ticket' means the average amount of money of each purchase.

LOCATION, LOCATION

You can handle a low footfall if all the customers are 'qualified', meaning that the people who come to the shop are very probably intending to buy something. That's why hobby stores, minority ethnic restaurants and other 'destination' retailers, which people specifically seek out, can make a living even in otherwise lousy locations. You can also handle low footfall and low purchase per customer if your average ticket size is huge – that's why sports car showrooms and jewellers can often make a go of surprisingly out-of-the-way locations. But for the majority of customer-oriented businesses, where a large proportion of the people in the shop are browsing rather than buying, and the average transaction size is small relative to the cost of turning the lights on and paying the staff, footfall is the big thing to be worrying about.

THE GRAVEYARD

In general, a graveyard site is one where the rent is too high for the footfall generated – the typical graveyard is a piece of space that's close enough to a desirable location on the main drag to have its rent per square foot pushed up to somewhere near its neighbours, but far enough off the pedestrian thoroughfares to have no meaningful passing trade. So how do these things ever get rented?

In many cases, the answer is because landlords of these premises will tend to offer an initial rent-free period. It makes sense to do this, because obviously a new business has set-up costs and will take some time to establish goodwill and repeat business, so it's more or less bound to be unprofitable and/or cash negative for the first few months. In principle, by including a rent-free period in the lease, the landlord is helping out with the cash flow problems and will benefit in the long term from a financially healthy tenant able to make payments and put up with rent rises.

CHARITY BEGINS ON A SIDE ROAD OFF THE HIGH STREET

In practice, it's all too common for someone who is just a little bit too optimistic about life (don't be too hard on them, economic progress fundamentally depends on the existence of such people) to take advantage of rent-free periods, suppliers' credit and all the other tricks and accommodations of the trade, to fundamentally overestimate the viability of the space and to set up a no-hoper business, which will trade for the rent-free period, then get into trouble pretty quickly and close down a few months later. Then there will be a void period, and the cycle will start again. The gaps between such tenants are the economic basis of charity shops.

RISK OF RENT CONTAGION

Note that this 'graveyard cycle' doesn't really work all that well for the landlord either – they are constantly going from rent-free period to void and back again, getting paid the agreed rent maybe one month in four if they are lucky. The sensible thing to do would be to lower the rent to a level where a business would be viable. But landlords will be reluctant to do this; lowering the rent on one of your sites tends to put pressure on a lot of the other ones, and there is always a bit of doubt as to whether a site is fundamentally unviable due to low footfall, or whether it's just had a run of bad luck with two or three Walter Mittyesque tenants. Added to which, there will often be financing on the site, which might have covenants or valuation clauses, which could be badly affected by a decision to reduce the rent, but which can always be finagled and renegotiated in cases of serial tenant turnover (certainly, if you're hoping to sell the site on, the last thing you want to be doing is cutting the ground rent). And the property industry itself is, shall we say, not wholly free of chancers and Mittys who are always dreaming of the perfect tenant just around the corner.

A DESTINATION BUSINESS

So the cycle often continues – usually until the site attracts a tenant who is 'right' for it, in being able to make one of the other parts of the retail equation work well enough to compensate for the poor footfall. Opposite the building we work in, there is a notorious graveyard site, which went through five or six family-restaurant tenants, until a specialist craft-beer company took it over and attracted a constant flow of qualified beer-buyers who came to the location specifically to go to that pub (and enough of whom are prepared to pay a 'ticket size' per pint, discussed on page 147, which could sensibly be regarded as positively insane).

Now business is booming and everyone is happy, especially one of the authors who sidles in to sample the products at least once a week.

WHY DO UNDERTAKERS LOOK LIKE FAMILY BUSINESSES, EVEN WHEN THEY AREN'T?

Some of the longest-lived businesses in the world are firms of funeral directors – the Queen Mother's funeral, for example, was arranged by Leverton & Sons of North London, which has been around since 1789. Funeral directors are also, somewhat unusually, still very likely to be family businesses that are handed down from generation to generation.

YOU DON'T SHOP AROUND WHEN YOU'RE DEAD

The reason for this is quite easy to understand – the funeral industry is one in which reputation is incredibly important. The purchasers of a funeral are usually in no state to be doing comparison shopping and so will tend to go for the first name that they can think of; in most cases, that will be the local undertaker who has done all the other funerals that the bereaved relatives have been to. From a business point of view, this means that it's very difficult for a start-up business to compete and gain customers. (Fascinating fact: one of the first automated telephone exchanges was invented by an undertaker called Almon Strowger, allegedly because he suspected that the wife of one of his competitors, who worked as an operator, was switching calls through to her husband's firm.)

THERE'S GOLD IN THEM THERE CORPSES

Given the importance of branding and reputation and the difficulty of competition, you would expect undertakers' businesses to earn very strong profit margins. And they do. Without going into the details, coffins are very, very expensive for what they are, and the service element is also very highly priced. In America (where it's common for corpses to be embalmed, and where metal 'caskets' are quite aggressively upsold), the average funeral cost is $6,600, plus cemetery costs, which can reach another several thousand. Even in the UK, Dignity plc, the quoted chain of funeral directors, gets an operating margin of around 30 per cent (£78.4m of underlying operating profit on £256m of revenues in 2013, its most recent set of accounts at the time of writing), which is pretty high; it's right up there with pharmaceutical companies and IT software firms.

Of course, there is something of a tension here; there is always considerable danger from a marketing point of view that the 'reputational capital' thing will end up clashing with the 'extremely profitable' thing. Although everyone must, at some level, realise that undertaking is a business and needs to make a profit (and actually, we'd argue, probably needs to make a very substantial profit if it's going to keep on getting successive generations of families into something that is hardly a glamour profession), it's a service industry that is based on some very powerful human emotions, so it's not a good idea to bring grieving customers face to face with anything that looks like a profit margin.

LOW-KEY BRANDING

That is why you don't tend to see much in the way of corporate branding on funeral parlours, even when they are actually owned by a corporate chain. The only funeral services company that we know of that makes a point of branding itself with its corporate identity is the Co-Op, and clearly they don't have the same issues when it comes to feelings of profiteering as a quoted company might.

What happens with other chains of funeral directors is that, when a family business comes to the end of the road (usually because the owner wants to retire and, for one reason or another, doesn't have an heir to pass the business on to), they sell out to another undertaker. This is how the chains typically are formed – Dignity and the Co-Op are the only two national chains in the UK, but there are quite a few local and regional operators. But you can't rebrand an undertaker as if it were a pub or a service station; what typically happens in these deals is, first, that the business name and goodwill are a large part of the purchase consideration, and, second, that the owner will be contracted to remain in place, on an 'earn-out' contract, which is often as long as five years (and can be even longer), to ensure that the transition to corporate ownership is smooth and that the local reputation isn't damaged.

ECONOMIES OF SCALE AREN'T DEAD

People who know about these things (such as the publishers of the *Good Funeral Guide*) reckon that it's often no bad thing when small local undertakers are bought out. For one thing, it's often better to have the business properly managed by people with a strong commercial interest in preserving the goodwill, rather than half-heartedly managed by a family member who never really wanted to be in the business and is only doing it out of a sense of duty. For another, there are genuine economies of scale, at least at a regional level, having the same mortuary facility shared between a number of undertakers – as happens in a lot of big cities where local chains have consolidated the industry – means that you can justify a lot more investment in facilities and skilled staff.

ECONOMIES OF SCALE

Some things are just more efficient to make in big units or large production runs. You can gain benefits of mass production (like Henry Ford) or spread out the fixed costs of making specialised tools. So, as your 'scale' increases, your average cost per unit falls. At some point, all the economies of scale are used up, and bigger production facilities become inefficient, as they need more management and overhead – this is why you sometimes hear about 'diseconomies of scale'.

RAISING THE DEAD

One other thing worth knowing about funeral chains is that the big corporate ones often tend to have quite a lot of debt. Because it's not a cyclical business and the revenues are really quite predictable from demographics, banks and private equity firms are typically willing to lend quite a lot against the cash flows, while the building up of a chain by acquiring family firms, by its nature, requires a lot of cash to be paid out the other side. Some industry observers (again, including the *Good Funeral Guide*) think that this consolidation has put considerable upward pressure on funeral costs over the last few years. So the moral of the story is, you probably can't get a better deal than from your local firm of undertakers, which is good to know at a time of serious stress. And, if it's good enough for the Queen Mother and Margaret Thatcher, it's probably good enough for you.

MONEY LAUNDERING

As they used to say at the end of kids' TV shows, 'Now, let's get serious, folks'. If there is only one piece of advice you take away from this book, it ought to be this – we really don't advise you get yourself in a situation where you are suspected of money laundering. As a business-destroying nightmare, it is only possibly equalled by 'getting yourself in a situation where you are suspected of VAT or excise fraud'.

DO NOT PASS GO, DO NOT COLLECT £200
The following things can get you seven years in jail – 1) money laundering; 2) helping someone else do money

laundering; 3) being aware that someone else is money laundering and not telling the authorities; and 4) being aware that someone else is money laundering, telling the authorities but tipping the person off that you have told the authorities. Basically, there is a world of pain here.

How might you find yourself in a situation where you might have to make an anti-money-laundering report if you don't work in a bank or similar institution? (If you do work in a bank or similar financial institution, you shouldn't need this book, because you will be getting your own regular anti-laundering training and our advice is to *pay attention*. Due to the aforementioned seven years in jail thing.)

CASH IS KING
Essentially, money laundering tends to work through the kinds of businesses that would have a plausible reason for being found in possession of large amounts of cash. So, restaurants and nightclubs are perfect contenders, such as, famously, pizza restaurants in New Jersey, which never seemed to have any customers in but always reported a roaring turnover. Football clubs used to be a great way to launder money in the days of standing terraces when it was impossible to be sure of attendance numbers. These days, a bookmaker with fixed-odds

betting terminals, or a fruit machine parlour, can find itself unwittingly used as a money laundry for street drug dealers – if someone comes in and loses ten per cent of their money on the one-armed bandits, then that can be considered a cheap price to pay in order to have the receipt that gives you a plausible explanation for why you've got a wedge of banknotes in your pocket if you get stopped and searched.

PARTNERSHIP WITH THE DEVIL

If you're involved with these sorts of businesses, then, seriously, make sure you trust everyone who has access to your banking arrangements. This sounds like amazingly obvious advice, but it's heartbreaking to see the occasional stories about people who thought they'd found the business partner from heaven – one who puts up some capital, handles all the paperwork, doesn't complain too much about not yet seeing a profit on their investment – who end up losing their business in forfeiture and having the fight of their lives to stay out of prison. And all because they hadn't realised that, if it's your name on the account, then it's your responsibility to make sure that everything that happens to that bank account is perfectly legal.

THE SECRET LIFE OF MONEY

TAKEN TO THE CLEANERS

So, if you are in a cash-generating business, make sure that all your finances are squeaky clean, so you don't find out, too late, that you've been used as a laundry business for someone else's dodgy dealings, and get taken to the cleaners.

Or, as the police call it, jail.

HOW MUCH DOES LIVING IN THE CATCHMENT AREA OF A GOOD SCHOOL DRIVE UP HOUSE PRICES?

How much does it add to the value of a house for it to be in the catchment area of a really good state school? If you're of a particular age, a particular social class and live in particular parts of particular cities, you might recognise this as the most stereotypical dinner-party question possible.

WHAT COST EDUCATION?
It's not difficult to see why a good state school catchment area could be a financial asset. Someone who is considering a choice between state and private education is making a pretty big purchasing decision; even bracketing out the

Etons and Harrows, private schools can run to £5,000 plus a term, out of post-tax income; over a seven-year secondary school career, that's sports car money. If you add in siblings, then you're talking over £200,000 to put two children through private secondary school, or over £300,000 for three little darlings. This doesn't so much add up to a high percentage of the value of a house, as add up to the price of a new house – the house that living in state school catchment area built.

BID UP

So, if two houses were otherwise wholly equal in their qualities, but one came with a guarantee of admission to a top-notch state school and the other was positioned so as to make it almost certain that the only state schools available were not so good, then presumably a certain kind of buyer – one that was absolutely certain about their family plans, absolutely certain that they would not move out of the area, and had enough income that they would be willing and able to pay for a private school if they couldn't get admission to a state school of a specific quality – could, in theory, be persuaded to bid up the price of the 'school-favoured' house by almost the entire amount of the aggregate school fee saving.

LOCATION, LOCATION

In practice, however, the bid-up effect is nothing like as much as this. If it were, we would expect housing in the catchment areas of popular schools to be entirely occupied by families with school-age children and by and large that isn't the case. Actually working out what the premium might be is a really tricky job, though, because the thought experiment of two 'otherwise identical houses' is rarely, if ever, found. Two houses with different school locations are in different *locations* – this factor is always the most important driver of house price differences – and so are likely to differ in a bunch of different ways. Furthermore, the differences are not going to be randomly distributed but will differ in a number of predictable ways. For example, the majority of good-school neighbourhoods are also good neighbourhoods in general, and so have a number of favourable characteristics, from green space, a thriving high street, lower levels of street crime, etc. Whereas poorer schools tend to be found in the kinds of neighbourhoods that have a host of other problems too, from the lack of local amenities, higher levels of crime, etc., and problems of these sorts are highly likely to drag down house prices.

This means that it is very difficult to tease out cause and effect and isolate the part of the price difference that is due only to proximity to a good school: there aren't a lot of matched pairs of physically similar houses in socio-demographically similar neighbourhoods, which only differ to the extent that one of those neighbourhoods is one of the very small minority of places that fit the description 'nice place with a lousy school'.

HEDONISM

So how do you work out the effect of proximity to a good school on house prices? The technique is known as 'hedonic regression'. This jargon term is easily unpacked and, yes, it does derive from the Greek word for pleasure, because it's so much fun doing the statistics on it. Or possibly, because the aim is to measure houses against criteria of what is pleasurable about them for their occupants. So, you compile a list of the different characteristics of houses in terms of the number of bedrooms, presence of a garage, location (right down to five digits of postcode, potentially, if you've got Tesco Clubcard sizes of dataset), size of garden, etc., etc. Having measured a load of different houses according to these criteria and so created an index of 'nice things about houses' in which each house ends up having a numerical value, you then carry out a 'regression' on the data.

A regression is a statistical process from which you can draw conclusions about the relationship between variables. So, in this case, you perform a regression comparing the 'niceness' index with 'prices' of each of the characteristics. The methodology – which we will not trouble you with here as to do so would involve writing two-thirds of a statistics textbook – basically tweaks the value of each characteristic, then computes the implied value of each house in the dataset, then sees how close this implied value is to the actual price, then goes back again and iterates until it's got a set of 'hedonic values' that is in some way globally the 'best fit'. In theory, the process would allow you to say how much value a square metre of garden adds to the price of a property, and how much living near a good state school adds.

THE UNCERTAINTY PRINCIPLE

That was, we admit, some pretty fast skating over some pretty gnarly statistics. And immediately, the sharp business brain will be coming up with a bunch of objections to the methodology and the conclusion. These could have to do with the quality of house price data (generally good, but with a long lag, meaning that the actual transaction prices can refer to different points in time of the sale being agreed on), the question of whether you can really add up characteristics this way to give a price of the full house (almost certainly not), and whether the uncertainty in the regression exercise is so big as to mean you can't have any confidence at all that a relatively minor characteristic like school proximity has been estimated correctly (usually you can't).

SMALLVILLE

All of these problems can be dealt with via a combination of using more sophisticated statistical techniques, using more data and, most importantly, tackling a less ambitious problem. So, for example, rather than estimating the value of a good state school across the whole country, say, we might want to estimate it for a single town. If you do that, you're going to have more of a chance of finding very similar houses that differ in respect of schools they gain entry to, increasing your ability to find a systematic pricing difference if it's there.

THE PRICE YOU PAY?

Many academics have attempted to put a price on proximity to good state secondary schooling, most recently in the academic article 'The price you pay', by Glen and Nellis (2010), who concluded that every 10 per cent point improvement in the pass rate in GCSE exams adds a price premium onto a house of between 1 and

3 per cent. So, if 90 per cent of pupils at school A pass their GCSEs, houses near it are likely to be 6–18 per cent more expensive than if the pass rate is only 30 per cent of pupils. However, it is clear that this price premium represents far less than the cost of equivalent private schooling for even one child; given that families usually have more than one child to put through school, we'd have expected the school premium to be much bigger if it was really doing the work. Therefore, we find that even this result doesn't really support the view that state schools are a really big driver of the variation in house prices. The reverse causation is much more likely to be the explanation – nice places have nice schools.

THE WIDER PRINCIPLES OF HEDONISM

By the way, the hedonic regression technique has much more general applications. The car industry, in particular, uses it a lot to try to guess what value the customer puts on things like sunroofs, metallic paint, different types of gearbox and so on. In general, if you're producing a product and aiming at a particular price point, you want to make it as attractive as possible to the customer, given a hard constraint on what it costs to make. Hedonic regression is one good way (although by no means the only one) to start thinking about how to do that. So, if you are starting up a business, before you go and see Duncan Bannatyne and the rest of the 'dragons', you might want to make sure you've crossed your 'i's and dotted your 't's on your hedonic regression charts.

Or maybe not.

'BLOOD DIAMONDS' AND THE MYSTERIOUS ABSENCE OF 'BLOOD EMERALDS'

With the Kanye West song 'Diamonds From Sierra Leone' in 2005 and a film titled *Blood Diamond* the following year, 2006 marked the high point in global awareness of the existence of 'conflict diamonds', and a campaign was launched for firm regulation in the international diamond trade in order to prevent money from diamond sales enriching warlords like Charles Taylor, or financing the bloody civil wars in Liberia and Sierra Leone. All of which is very noble, but rather curious – because the civil wars had already ended in both countries in 2002–03, and by 2006 Charles Taylor himself was imprisoned in the Hague awaiting trial on charges of crimes against humanity. Liberia had signed the peace agreement officially ending the war in 2003, and by 2005 it was holding its first democratic election. The civil war was resolved even earlier in Sierra Leone, officially coming to an end in 2002, when a Truth and Reconciliation Commission was established, and elections for a new government were held. Between 2002 and 2007, the government of Sierra Leone, with significant assistance from the British government, implemented a major programme of economic and state rebuilding, which led up to a set of democratic elections in 2007, which were described by impartial observers as free and fair.

All of which meant that the international campaign against 'conflict diamonds' was effectively encouraging people to deprive a fledgling African democracy of one of its most important sources of hard currency revenue. What was going on?

KIMBERLEY

Well, 2005 was the third year of operation of the 'Kimberley Process Certification Scheme'. This required diamond producers and traders to sign up to a code of conduct which was meant to prevent conflict states, or brutal undemocratic leaders like Charles Taylor, from being able to sell their diamonds. Additionally, the Kimberley Process signatories laser-etched their diamonds with an identifying mark, enabling consumers to be sure that there was no chance at all of their precious stones being blood diamonds.

In principle, this was not a bad idea. It marked a turning point, in which the diamond industry, rather unusually in its history, decided that it didn't in fact want to do business with some of the worst people on earth. However, it turned out that the Kimberley Process was highly problematic, and Global Witness, the NGO that had launched the 'Blood Diamonds' campaign in the first place, disavowed it in 2011, claiming it had failed in its purpose and that it did not provide consumers with assurance that diamonds are not 'blood diamonds'. Global Witness went on to say that the Kimberley Process could not work as long as governments no longer continued to show an interest in reform.

RESTRICTING THE SUPPLY

So what went wrong? A key part of the problem is that the Kimberley Process was always designed to be a 'supply-restricting licensing scheme', a system whereby the supply of a good is artificially restricted. This clearly generates a cartel of 'correct', i.e. licensed, producers, and once you have a cartel of an artificially restricted supply you have a system that tends towards keeping prices high.

> ## CARTEL
> An agreement between companies in an industry to fix prices, usually by keeping supply lower than the amount that could really be produced. The practice is usually illegal.

We are cynical to believe this could have had some effect on the industry and diamond-producing governments getting on board with the Kimberley Process. Because the real issue is – diamonds aren't really very rare. Sure, they are uncommon, they don't grow on trees. But they do grow in massive diamond mines all over the world. But the whole diamond industry has been set up from the days of Cecil Rhodes to control the scarcity of diamond supply and to maintain the producers' cartel. The power of this cartel was looking problematic in the early 2000s as further huge diamond mines were discovered and exploited in Botswana and Russia. The Russians had their own way of dealing with the problem of over-supply: in 2009, President Putin ordered the Russian government to buy $1bn in uncut diamonds from the country's largest mine in order to support the country's diamond industry.

KEEPING UP THE CARTEL

But not all countries had this option, so the Kimberley Process was just the ticket as far as the producers were concerned. It kept prices high by keeping supply artificially restricted; while the initial certifications were being agreed, several large producers effectively lost access to a large part of the Western jewellery market, which is of course the most lucrative place for diamonds to be sold. The Kimberley Process didn't just cut out terrorists and dictatorships; it also cut out anyone who wasn't able to comply with a really quite detailed and bureaucratic licensing process. It made sure that nearly all the rough diamonds in the world continued to be sold onto the market via a small number of state-controlled producer monopolies. And, of course, nobody went around historically certifying the second-hand diamond market as Kimberley Process-compliant, i.e. checking if all the second-hand diamonds out there were, or were not, 'blood diamonds'. So the process opened up the potential to create a pricing premium for newly mined diamonds – keeping a lid on the second-hand market is a big priority for the diamond cartel. In general, producers of commodity goods with doubtful scarcity value and a very difficult management problem in sustaining a super-premium price ... these guys love their bureaucratic and complex licensing schemes. (Cynics say similar things about Fairtrade and the various 'Organic' labelling organisations.)

IT'S HARD TO BE DIAMOND IN A RHINESTONE WORLD

So the producers have it easy under the Kimberley Process, but, if it prevents mining of new 'blood diamonds' nevertheless, what's not to like? The problem is that it didn't, not sufficiently for Global Witness and other well-intentioned NGOs and campaigners to stand by it. It was found that some diamond mines whose proceeds went to innocent parties – if international diamond-mining companies are innocent – were unable to meet certification standards. It was also found that a diamond mine could be well run, and able to tick all the bureaucratic boxes to gain certification, but the proceeds could still be used to fuel conflict and oppression. In addition, smuggling into a market so full of non-licensed second-hand diamonds was easy – it is estimated that the diamonds smuggled from Sierra Leone alone amounted to four times the amount of legally exported diamonds between 2001 and 2006. Jay Z said, 'I thought my Jesus piece was so harmless, till I saw a picture of a shorty armless.' But, as a means of preventing this link, the Kimberley Process just didn't work.

BLOOD WILL HAVE BLOOD

We can see that there was a degree of producer interest in the 'Blood Diamond' publicity material from simply observing that emeralds, rubies and sapphires are also produced by some of the nastiest regimes in the world. But emeralds and rubies are actually rare (or, at least, a lot rarer than diamonds), and so there's much less call for anyone to invent means of artificially creating scarcity. So this is why you don't see any certification schemes or awareness-raising internet videos about the 'Blood Rubies' dug up by slave labour in Myanmar. Or, for that matter, much in the way of campaigning about 'Blood PlayStations' and 'Blood iPhones', which use significant amounts of tantalum in their manufacture, an ore that is mined in a lot of sites of civil wars in Africa.

The fight against these blood minerals is something that we need the Greenpeaces and Friends of the Earth and Green Parties of this world to lead on, without expecting too much help from rappers, film-makers, or the industries themselves producing them.

LEARNING CURVES AND WHY PEOPLE DON'T NECESSARILY DO WHAT'S GOOD FOR THEM

It's possible to cook yourself nutritious meals for less than £2 a day; nutritionists prove it, there are any number of recipe books to show it, and, from time to time, government ministers or secret millionaires will pop up on reality TV shows to demonstrate that it really, truly is the case. So why do so many people on limited incomes buy ready-meals and fast food when it's so obviously a very bad use of their food budget? The answer is often complex and multi-layered, and has much to do with societal pressures, low self-esteem and other things that are tough to change. But there is also another clear reason, which is the one we will deal with here, which is that it is because they don't know how to cook. But this only invites the next question, which is – since it would be so clearly financially advantageous to be able to cook, why not learn?

One aspect of the answer has to do with a concept that often comes in very handy when looking at all kinds of businesses, particularly small ones – the concept of a learning curve, the cost of moving up it and the ability to manage bad outcomes. In actual fact, thinking about why single mums in council flats don't learn to cook nutritious meals from cheap ingredients will give you a reasonable insight into why manufacturing companies with bank loan facilities often fall behind the technology curve and go out of business, because the basic economic phenomenon is the same.

HELL'S KITCHEN

The trick is this: part of the cost of learning to cook is making mistakes. And that, in a nutshell, is why it's so much easier to learn to cook if you've got even a little bit of spare income, versus learning to cook when you're at the level of poverty where it's really important to be able to cook. Throwing away a failed dish or a successful dish that your children utterly refuse to eat is a laugh and an anecdote when all it means is that you phone out for pizza; when it means throwing away your only hot meal of the day, it's a much worse prospect. And so it's not surprising that people on very limited incomes don't start on this project; they are much worse equipped to deal with the resulting inevitable uncertainty.

So, our advice would be: learn to cook for yourself before you go through any major life crises. When the chips are down, you may be extremely glad that you did.

BUSINESS HELL

It's similar for small businesses. No matter how high the return on investment on a new piece of equipment or a new process, it's no good if you go bankrupt before you're able to enjoy it. And any change to a business is going to have upfront costs – the purchase price of the machine itself, the inevitable disruption while it's installed and the staff are retrained, and, usually, a period of time when the new process is running well below peak efficiency and often somewhat worse than the old one it replaced. Unless you've got cash in the bank (both literally, and in terms of your relationships with your clients), it's a huge risk to change anything that seems to be working right now, even if failing to do so is the surest path to failure in the long run.

FIX THE ROOF WHILE THE SUN SHINES

All of which implies that the task of any individual person, or individual business, is always to be looking ahead and planning for the future. It isn't good enough in the life of any person or company to look after your, or your customers', needs now. You also need to anticipate what they may be in different circumstances in the future.

Life-long learning is a much laughed-at phrase, but, to prevent the financial dangers associated with sharp learning curves, it has a lot to recommend it.

KENYAN FLOWERS

On the face of it, it would seem to make no sense whatsoever for fresh flowers and cut vegetables to be flown in from farms in Kenya to make an appearance in British supermarkets every day. It's true that Kenya has a number of advantages over the UK as a place to grow fresh produce, and a considerable comparative advantage in labour costs when it comes to tasks like stringing and washing mange tout, or cutting and arranging flowers, but these commodities have a fairly low value-density and air freight is pretty expensive. Indeed, anyone who cares about 'food miles' is likely to view the practice of transporting fruit, flowers and vegetables thousands of miles by aeroplane as obscenely wasteful, even if it does allow British consumers to eat mangoes, and have roses on their table, out of season.

But it's actually a little more complicated than that. Consider this – what if you had a plane that was going from Kenya to the UK anyway? Say because it had been taking air freight from Britain to Kenya, and the plane was now needed back in Heathrow to take a load somewhere else? Wouldn't it be less wasteful to fill it up with at least something that had a guaranteed market in Britain, rather than sending it back totally empty?

BACKLOADS

Of course it would. And indeed, an awful lot of the food and flowers that come into the UK from Africa are in fact sent as 'backloads', so it's not obvious what the true carbon footprint of the packaged cut vegetables in your supermarket really is. The marginal cost of sending a plane full of vegetables versus sending it back empty is pretty small too, which is why Kenyan agricultural exporters can get freight rates low enough to make the whole enterprise economically viable.

A SUFFICIENT LOAD OF BACKLOADS?

In fact, there probably wouldn't be anything like enough two-way backload traffic between Kenya and Britain to haul in all of the fruit and vegetable exports this way.

But Kenya gets air-freighted imports from all over the world – for mail if nothing else – and it only exports cut flowers and packaged vegetables to a few countries, all of them major transport hubs like the UK. Wherever a freight plane has come from, it's almost always going to be a sensible idea to send it to London to find a cargo, so the Kenya–UK export trade can effectively pick up backloads from nearly all of the incoming air-freight traffic, not just the planes that are literally flying back and forth between London and Nairobi. In fact, backloads are so important to the whole trade that their availability has been identified by the World Bank as a serious constraint on the expansion of the Kenyan (and Tanzanian) agriculture industries. It can also be potentially quite ruinous for small producers in these countries when they have a fixed-supply contract with a major retailer and, for one reason or another, they find that there is a shortage of backload traffic and, for the sake of the contract, they have to pay full freight cost, losing a ton of money on the shipment to do so.

MARGINAL COST

Backloads are one of the features of the global shipping and freight market that make its economics fairly impenetrable to outsiders (anyone using the Baltic Dry

Index as an index of anything other than the marginal cost of chartering a certain kind of ship in London, for example, is highly likely to be kidding themselves). This is because the marginal cost can be so very, very different from the average cost (one of the Big Ideas, see 'The afterlife of money'), which is often a source of apparently crazy business behaviour.

AIR FREIGHT

Backloads aren't completely ubiquitous, by the way – Britain doesn't export many of the kinds of manufactured goods that arrive at Southampton in container ships from China, so it's probably true to say that, by volume, our biggest bilateral export is container loads of nice fresh South Coast air.

SAFE AS HOUSES

'You can't go wrong with bricks and mortar,' the staple of dinner party bore investment advice, which will be familiar to most people in Britain. In actual fact, and in long runs of data, bricks and mortar (in the sense of residential house prices) are neither particularly high return nor particularly low risk. Over nearly every investment time period you might name, they are outperformed by investments in the stock market. Yes, honestly. Look at the chart below if you don't believe us:

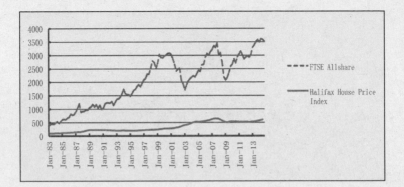

So what is it about bricks and mortar that, despite the data to the contrary, has made it so very attractive to so many investors?

EVERYONE'S GOT TO LIVE SOMEWHERE

There are obvious reasons and ... less obvious reasons. So we will dispense with the obvious ones pretty quickly because they're the least interesting. One useful technical property of housing as a retirement investment is that it's got very favourable correlation properties with your consumption needs in retirement – in other words, when you're retired, you're still going to want to live in a house, and so it is good to have an investment that will go up in value, especially if 'living in a house' turns out to be more expensive than you thought it was going to be.

ULYSSES TIED TO THE MAST

Another useful fact about housing (if purchased with a mortgage) is that it's a form of compulsory saving. If you're a little bit worried about your own willpower when it comes to saving, it's nice to have an arrangement whereby you do some of your long-term saving every month in the same payment as the one you make for your housing costs. It's like Ulysses asking to be tied to the mast of his boat so that he would be unable to follow the sirens' calls and jump into the water to his death.

DO YOU TRUST A UNIT TRUST?

But ... these correlation, and compulsion, arguments don't work well at all to explain the appeal of the buy-to-let market. Rather, the arguments only really apply to owner-occupied housing, and not always very strongly there – there are lots of cases in which, on pure investment grounds, people would be better off renting rather than buying, and putting the saving in the cost of rent-versus-buy into a low-cost unit trust. (By the way, if there isn't any financial benefit from renting rather than buying – i.e. mortgage payments are lower than rent – then that's generally a very strong sign that house prices are going to go up. But we can't all live in such rare and favourable times.)

Part of the attraction of all bricks and mortar investments, whether you live in one of them or rent it out, is, of course, the immense and accelerating lack of trust in the financial services sector, which makes any major investment that does not come from the mouths of banking advisers and IFAs seem like a good one. But we believe there is a further appeal of housing as an investment, which is possibly more dubious.

SAFE AS DUCK HOUSES

What is really attractive about bricks and mortar to many people, in our view, is that it's one of the few forms of leveraged investment available to the common man or woman. Leveraged investment means investment using debt. Mortgages are debt, and therefore by borrowing money to buy a house using a mortgage you are using a leveraged investment product. And often quite a highly leveraged product – a bank will often lend mortgages with only a 20 per cent deposit, which is another way of saying that you are borrowing at a leverage of 5 to 1 (20 per cent vs 100 per cent). Other forms of leveraged investment products are not usually available to your average Joanna in the street – you have to be pretty rich these days to find a stockbroking firm that will let you buy stocks with borrowed money, in what they call a 'margin account'. And, even in that case, the leverage you can generate is pretty low, unless you are spread betting (which is a different kettle of fish altogether and is not even as safe as proverbial duck houses). Whichever way you go about it, margin accounts will typically see you paying through the nose, which compares very unfavourably to a mortgage offered by a bank at some of the very lowest interest rates available on any kind of loan.

MARGIN CALL

And compared to a speculator's margin account, mortgage debt is a very benign form of leverage, because it's not 'call money'. Call money works in this way: if you are losing money in a margin account on your leveraged stock investment (or your spread bet), then the bank will ask you to put cash in to top it up, and very quickly too. If you can't find the cash to do so, then the position will be closed out for you, which could result in your taking a heavy loss. So it's pretty difficult to ride out the bumps in a margin account, unless you have access to a lot of spare cash – in which case, why didn't you just buy more stock in the first place?

LACK OF FORECLOSURE

FORECLOSURE

To foreclose on a company is to declare it bankrupt, then move in and take ownership of the assets to try to get back some of the money it owes you. There are fairly complicated rules about who is allowed to foreclose, what they are allowed to do with the assets and what agreements they have to get from other creditors.

A mortgage, on the other hand, has a twenty-five-year term and a monthly payment. The bank might wish it could do something to foreclose early if the value of your house falls (which increases their exposure), but in general it can't, unless you miss a payment. Even if you do, foreclosure is a lengthy process, giving you the maximum number of chances to wait your way out of negative equity. If your investment goes into profit, however, you can sell out quickly, usually with only a relatively small prepayment penalty.

EXPOSURE

The total amount that somebody (or some company, or some government) owes to you is your 'exposure' to that 'counterparty'. It's the maximum amount you stand to lose if they go bust.

LEVERAGE UP

All this isn't a good reason to do buy-to-let, by the way – it's axiomatic (and actually mathematically provable – Modigliani and Miller won the Nobel Prize for this one) that leverage can't turn a bad investment into a good one or vice versa. But, if you find yourself at a point on the risk tolerance spectrum where you fancy a bit of leverage, residential property investment offers it on much more favourable terms than most other kinds. And that in a nutshell is why we believe the buy-to-let market has gone so radio rental mental in recent years – it's most people's one route to doubling up big time. And even if it all goes wrong, and a housing crash strikes and plunges buy-to-letters into negative equity, there is the option to sit and wait it out, something you simply can't do in other leveraged investments.

HITSVILLE UK – WHY IS A RECORD LABEL LIKE A PHARMACEUTICAL COMPANY?

So, what do record labels have in common with oil prospectors and pharmaceutical companies? Basically, that in all three of these industries, a large part of their revenues comes from a small number of 'hits', while a large part of the costs comes from an endless sequence of projects that didn't quite work out. If you measure only the successful efforts – the hit records, wonder drugs and productive oilfields – then you get a wholly misleading impression of the profitability of all three industries, because part of the cost of coming up with a Coldplay or One Direction is the promotion and recording of a couple of dozen wannabes. Similarly, dry holes are part of the cost of drilling oil wells, while the pharmaceutical industry is prepared to tolerate even lower hit rates; it's not uncommon to test literally hundreds of compounds in preliminary (but still highly expensive) studies for every drug that makes it to market.

It's this dependence on hits that makes these kinds of industries such a total pain to analyse – if you're ever called on to do consultancy work for one of them, it is not very much fun at all to spend a few weeks finding out that the problem is 'not enough hits' and that you are going to be faced with giving a presentation the essence of which boils down to 'try to have a few hits'. John Paul Getty apocryphally gave advice to a young man who had written to him, which went: 'Rise early. Go to bed early. Work hard. Strike oil', but he could get away with it.

THE ONLY WAY IS BIG

What companies tend to do is the only thing that you really can do if your entire industrial driver is basically a risk management problem – get bigger. For the same reason that there are few 'mom and pop' insurance companies, there is an almost irresistible tendency for companies in the media, pharmaceutical and extractive sectors to consolidate. Basically, the bigger you are, the likelier it is that there will be something going right in some part of your business, and the nature of hits-based industries is that a couple of big cash generators (Madonna, or Viagra, or the Spindletop well in Texas, for example) will pay a lot of bills elsewhere. The other advantage of being big is that, if you're big and adequately capitalised (by which we mean, you haven't taken on a stupid amount of debt), you can usually last out longer periods of famine than if you're small.

FALLING OFF THE CLIFF

Bigness and diversity also allow you more scope in managing the life-cycle of a hits-based business. In all three of the industries we mentioned, there is a finite period during which you can extract value from even the best ideas. This is determined by geology in the case of oil wells, by the patent lifespan in biotechnology and by the inevitable cycle of cool and uncool in media and games industries. By the nature of things, a bigger company can have more projects on the go, at different stages of maturity, so it doesn't suffer from 'cliff' problems when its cash cow dries up. Having said that, this tends to work more in principle than in practice – even giant pharmaceutical companies can have patent cliffs, simply because monster drugs are so hugely profitable when they're in patent.

WHAT'S IN THE PIPELINE?

Growth and acquisition apart, the key thing to look at when you're thinking about a hits-based business is the 'pipeline' of ideas in development. This is the key management report to look at in this kind of industry, and what you want to see is a lot of credible ideas, at varying stages of development, with sufficient resources to bring them all (or a good proportion of them) to fruition. Instead, what you often actually see are companies that have been put up for sale on the basis of one or two big current hits, with a pipeline that consists of nothing but early-stage speculative proposals. In our experience, these are situations that you should run from, not walk; almost invariably, they're a sign of a company that has had one big success, then poured all of its effort into building on that success, then realised that they're going to reach a cliff, and then piled on a load of new, often terrible, ideas in order to dress up the pipeline in the hope of selling the business.

CAN SMALL BE BEAUTIFUL?

This isn't to say that there's no place in the world for small record labels, biotechnology companies or oil prospectors – just that the long-term future for successful small firms in this kind of industry tends to be an acquisition by a bigger player, rather than anything else. The smaller players tend to be single-idea companies, based on a single drug, a small number of bands or a licence to explore in a particularly hairy part of the world (there are quite a few mining companies, for example, that maintain stock-market quotes based on licences for parts of Afghanistan where there are believed to be valuable minerals, but where no geologist, no matter how drunk or suicidal, can be persuaded to go out and check). If everyone (including their financial advisers) is doing their job properly, these companies are bought out at just the right stage – when the drug goes into final testing, or the seismic studies prove the reserves, or the band strikes its first radio hit – when the major player's better financial resources can cope with the investment needed to bring the hit to full scale.

GENETIC SCREENING AND HEALTH INSURANCE

Every now and then, you read in the newspaper that, in the relatively near future (usually 'the next 20 years'), people will be genetically tested at birth for all the ailments that they might be susceptible to. This is usually the occasion for a bit of journalistic handwringing about how the poor souls who are given the genetic 'black spot' are ever going to get life assurance, but, in reality, we should not be so worried. In general, the people making these predictions seem to know a lot more about genetics and health than they do about insurance.

We are not going to definitively say that no such thing will ever be possible in any factual or science-fictional world, but would definitely say with high confidence that the derivation of commercially relevant and actionable insurance information from genetics is much, much more difficult than people think. Furthermore, we would tentatively advance the possibility that to 'accurately assess the cost of medical treatment over a lifetime' might end up being at least as much of a tough-nut as forecasting the entire progress of technology over the next fifty years.

THE TITANIC PROBLEM

The big issue here is what we might call the 'Titanic problem' (from Hitchcock's aphorism about it being possible to make a suspenseful film about the *Titanic* even though everyone knows that it sinks – they don't know when). Similarly, knowing that someone has a genetic propensity to develop various conditions is just one tiny baby step along the way to making a cost estimate of the sort described. Just reeling off the other forecasting fun from the top of our heads, if you were actually going to take the magic genetic test that is apparently only a few years in the future, and use it as an input into calculating an actuarially fair premium, you'd need answers to the following questions:

1) How long will it take for the condition to develop? (or, how many years' premiums will the punter have

plugged in before they get the disease and make a claim?)

2) How much will the condition cost to treat when they get it?

3) How does your answer to 2) depend on your estimate of medical cost inflation?

4) How does your answer to 2) depend on your assumptions about technological progress in medicine – given that we are talking about thirty- or forty-year horizons at a minimum here?

5) How do your answers to 3) and 4) interact, given that technological progress can either facilitate the prolongation of late-stage care at massive expense, or make hugely debilitating conditions curable with a twenty-dollar appliance?

6) How do the genetic markers interact; what is the possibility that a marker for a profitable condition (ideally, one that kills the insured stone dead with no warning after having paid a lifetime's premiums) is correlated with an unprofitable one?

7) How will the customer's estimates of 1–6, plus your terms and premiums, affect their behaviour and so their propensity to have more, or less, healthy lives?

MEDICAL RISK VERSUS FINANCIAL RISK

This looks totally impossible to us. Question 4) is the real killer because long-term forecasts of technical progress in medical science are pretty close to impossible. You can get an awful lot of information about *medical* risk to the *customer* and still be in a state of close to perfect ignorance about the *financial* risk to the *insurer*.

RISK POOLING AND STANDARD TERMS

However, wonderful, wonderful mathematics provides an easy way out of this one. The mathematics of risk pooling is the closest thing to a free lunch you are ever going to get. Because, although the Titanic problem is massive, you can be sure close to certainty that the Grim Reaper is going to play that Celine Dion song to all of us, sooner or later. If you give up on price-discrimination, then what you are modelling is the average outcome for the average patient, and this is a much easier thing to do than modelling a specific outcome for a specific patient. Even today, given all that we know about health outcomes (compared with

132

what we knew in the eighteenth century when the first life assurance companies were founded), nearly all life assurance business is written on standard terms. Apart from a small number of genetic conditions and HIV, the only thing that makes a real difference is the connection between cigarette smoking and lung cancer; smokers can buy special annuity products that pay higher retirement benefits because it's expected that the client will collect them for a shorter term. Otherwise, the life assurance industry prefers to work by gathering us all together in a big pool and assuming, on good evidence, that the good and the bad will balance each other out.

RISK PRICING FLAMEOUTS

In general, standard terms and risk pooling are proven technology. They work, and they have worked for about 250 years, give or take. Risk pricing, risk management and discrimination have a much shorter history and have caused quite a few spectacular flameouts for their users in their short existence. Really the only exception to this rule was the invention of standard terms themselves – the compilation of the first mortality tables worked straight from the off, and quickly did for the previous model of life assurance (fraternal benefits societies, like the Odd Fellows, who didn't use mortality tables and were therefore very vulnerable to the disastrous financial effects of an aging membership). Other than that, the history of price discrimination in long-term insurance is pretty wretched; where the average policy has very few claims, the concept of a no-claims bonus doesn't make much sense.

GENETIC TESTING – A THREAT NOT AN OPPORTUNITY

A footnote: we think that a lot of people also get misled on this one by the observable fact that the insurance industry does in fact take a very strong interest in genetic markers and prognosis, and funds a lot of research into them. This is not really because they have some dream of hunting down the chimera of perfect price discrimination though, but because they're worried about good old-fashioned adverse selection; they're worrying about the patients having an information edge over them. If you have good information about the likelihood and timing of something happening to you, you can load up on coverage and effectively use your insurance policy as a low-cost savings vehicle, to the considerable expense of your insurer. Genetic testing (and this ought to be obvious lly, given that the basis of insurance is risk pooling) is at to health insurance, not an opportunity.

CLAIMS MANAGEMENT –
DIY FOR THE WIN

INERTIA

A surprising amount of economic activity is based on the fact that, when faced with a significant benefit in return for a token amount of effort, a large proportion of the population can't be bothered or don't get round to it. We're all aware of this in our own lives, but there are people out there who have built it into their pricing models. Electrical goods with 'rebates' that nobody bothers to claim, the vast float of never-to-be-claimed air miles – even the government will often include in its estimates of the cost of a particular benefits programme the fact that a material proportion of the people entitled to the benefit will not get around to claiming it (this is the ultimate false economy, as, in general, the hardship suffered by the people failing to claim the overly complex benefit will end up showing up as a major problem somewhere else in the system, but Treasury accounting doesn't tend to pick this up).

The inertia industry supports a few rather weirder businesses though – the ones that are dedicated to effectively arbitraging the pricing policies that depend on customer inertia and trying to make a profit out of the money that we, the consumer, leave on the table. The most prominent examples are the 'claims management' companies, the ones that advertise so aggressively through phone spam and on daytime television.

LAWYERS AND REBATES

Take a moment to think about your friends. Which of them seem to have the persistence and organisational skill to claim every rebate to which they're entitled, pay all their bills on time to take advantage of discounts, switch their credit card balance at the end of the introductory offer period, and so on? If your friends are like ours, it's generally the lawyers and accountants. On the other hand, if you think about who might be pretty bad at iming things to which they're entitled, it's confused, rable people. And by their nature, confused and vulnerable people tend to often be entitled to payouts from compensation settlements, simply because they tend to be the kind of people who have compensation-worthy things done to them more often than the rest of us. And compensation settlements tend to be agreed by lawyers. It's a match made in heaven.

BUILDING UP THE CLAIMS SETTLEMENT BUSINESS

What you tend to see from time to time (and these types of business tend to grow up in waves) is that a hard-working and entrepreneurial solicitor wins a few similar cases for their clients, and then grows to realise that the three or four cases they have litigated are the tip of a much larger iceberg. From this realisation, it is only a short step to working out that, if you standardise and industrialise the claims process, then you can build an entirely viable business around taking your fees or your share of the settlements, as long as you can find enough cases to feed the legal pipeline that you've created. Of course, people who are entitled to compensation but haven't claimed it tend to be quite well blessed when it comes to inertia, and so you have to advertise pretty aggressively in order to find them, but if you have a thick skin, you can make a very profitable business out of it. In the last few years, we've seen this happen with PPI mis-selling, personal injury claims, industrial deafness and even with people who should have been declaring a form of bankruptcy on their credit card debts, but who wouldn't have bothered to get round to it unless advised by one of the 'Debt Counselling' firms that used to advertise. Some of the debt counselling firms even made it as far as a stock-market quote, although most investors lost their shirts.

WHAT GOES AROUND COMES AROUND

The reason why this kind of business is usually not a good long-term investment is that it's very dependent on another form of inertia – the business inertia in the large corporations that it's claiming from. In general, the source of funds is an insurance company or a bank, or some other entity with deep pockets that has, in some way or another, incurred a large aggregate liability to a large number of small claimants. What companies tend to do when they find themselves in this position is to set up a claims management process, which is aimed at settling the whole messy affair for the smallest possible administrative cost. Scrutinising and fighting every single claim is usually bad business; it's bad for the brand, it costs a lot of money to do and, in the early days at least, you tend to lose nearly all of the cases, because the nature of these things is that the first cases to be brought tend to be the strongest ones, with the most motivated claimants.

In the early stages at least, a policy of settling claims without much fuss tends to be the best course of action, not least because the corporations are able to rely on our old friend inertia – the marginal and lower-quality cases, which it might be worthwhile to fight against, don't tend to be brought at all, because the claimants can't be bothered. What happens when a system set up in this way bumps into an aggressive set of lawyers who have built their business around it? Nothing good for the corporation involved, and, if you ever have the opportunity to see the panic created when the claims volume suddenly goes through the roof, it is quality entertainment. This is the period – after the claims process has been industrialised, but when the settlement infrastructure is still working on the old basis – when serious money is made in the claims-handling industry, and it tends to be the point at which some of them are floated.

YOU'LL GET WHAT'S COMING TO YOU...

The trouble is, if your business model is based on the assumption that large companies can't get their act together, you are very vulnerable to the possibility that those same large companies might, after a while, get their act together. This is what tends to happen to claims management industries – the big companies that they are claiming from realise what's happening and tighten up their processes, usually in a co-ordinated fashion. The other failure mode of claims management companies is that, although some of them are perfectly ethical and charge reasonable fees, they tend to be plagued by rogue operators who just 'farm' claimants, paying them a token amount and keeping an unfair share of the profit for themselves. Even the best ones aren't that good – you are almost always best off going through the minor hassle yourself and making an early claim – but, of course, that's easier to advise than to do!

RANDOM NUMBERS
THAT AIN'T

The financial mathematician and derivatives expert Paul Wilmott occasionally tries an experiment on his audiences of trainee derivatives mathematicians ('quants', in the jargon, from 'quantitative analysts') to gauge their level of market savvy. It revolves around describing a magic trick in which you name a card – say, the Ace of Hearts – and the magician shuffles the pack and turns over the top card. What's the probability, Paul Wilmott asks, that the card the magician turns over will be the Ace of Hearts? There's a kind of hierarchy of the answers given:

'1 in 52.'

Terrible. You even forgot about the jokers.

'1 in 54.'

Also terrible. You really think that the magician is going to go through all that then draw a card at random?

'100 per cent.'

Quants usually give this answer (financial regulators usually, and quite frighteningly, not only give one of the 'random number' answers but also vigorously argue that it is the 'correct' one because manipulating the cards is cheating!). This answer is not quite as bad as it could be, but in fact it is still a fairly unsophisticated response.

'Slightly less than 100 per cent.'

Good, you took into account that the magician might have messed up. This might be right in a lot of situations. But we'd hope that the very best brains would at least consider...

'Close to zero.'

Come on, this is a professional magician. Is the trick really going to be something as simple and unimpressive as turning over a named card after a single 'shuffle'? Maybe if you're watching your nephew's magic show, or the magician is not actually doing a performance and you're watching them practise their card mechanics. But, in general, the point here is that actually thinking about the card trick in terms of probabilities is a sure-fire route to getting confused. Because this isn't a random process; it looks like one, but it's actually a completely deterministic process, which you don't understand.

So the correct answer to give is more like…

'I refuse to give an answer in the form of a probability, because, despite being set up to look like one, this is not really a probability question.'

I GO BACK TO BLACK

Here is a similar example, about which we've also had stand-up shouting-match arguments with derivative quants. A roulette wheel has just come up on 32-black seven times out of the last ten spins. What should you bet on?

Anyone who has taken a course in probability is absolutely going to argue that it doesn't matter which number you bet on, and that it's the 'gambler's fallacy' to think either that 32-black is on a winning streak, or that it all has to 'even out' with a longer period of no 32-blacks. But that's because they're thinking of the imaginary, abstract and perfectly random roulette wheel that probability textbooks often ask you to imagine when they want to liven up a boring problem set. Not a physical roulette wheel, the kind you get in an actual casino.

CASINO ROYALE

If a physical roulette wheel comes up on the same number seven times out of ten, then it is possible that this is a massive coincidence. But it's also very possible that the roulette wheel has something wrong with it; perhaps its mechanical floor has malfunctioned, or it's not levelled properly, or someone has fiddled with it. Statistics profs will tell you that, in a sample of 10,000 spins, you're bound to get some runs of consecutive numbers, purely by chance. But in the real world, there are actually people who will do 10,000 spins of the same roulette wheel and write down the results. They work for the casinos, and they're called 'technical managers', and a large part of their job is to make sure that the equipment is working properly and hasn't developed any funny biases, through accident or (usually more relevantly and certainly more worryingly for the casino) cheating.

THE MAN WHO LOST HIS SHIRT AT MONTE CARLO

So, how should you bet on the hypothetical roulette wheel? Certainly, there's a case to be made for 32-black. But on full reflection, we'd say that there's a chance that this roulette wheel is being fiddled, and fiddled by a gang who are both technically pretty incompetent (because they can only stick the ball in one number) and not very bright (because they're banging down the same number at a frequency that's bound to get them noticed). It could be that the wheel is just broken, in which case the casino will probably, but not necessarily, honour your winning bets. But it would be just our luck to have security come by and drag everyone who had put money down on 32-black into the back room, for the kind of evening that could spoil your whole holiday.

We'd take it as a sign to gather up our chips and walk off to catch the magic show.

CRAFTY BREWERS

Anyone who drinks beer and is at least vaguely aware of fashions and trends will have heard of, or even drunk, 'craft beer' at some point in the recent past. And while savouring the complex flavour and perhaps reading about the interesting back story of the small specialist brewer responsible, you might have asked yourself a question that comes up frequently in any discussion of this emerging drinks industry trend – why is the stuff so incredibly expensive?

And expensive it is; the Brewdog chain of brewery-owned pubs are regularly willing to charge £4.95 for a third-of-a-pint glass of one of their more ferociously alcoholic concoctions. Given that a pint is 568ml, the implied price for a 70cl bottle would be £18.30. That's not quite the cost of malt whisky or vintage champagne, but it's significantly more than an average bottle of wine.

THE GRAPES OF WRATH

Yet wine ought to be more expensive than beer, for a variety of reasons. First, it's aged, and so it has a capitalised interest cost element to it. Second, it's an agricultural product rather than an industrial one. This means that supply is limited in a number of ways; a wine producer can't ramp up production if they have a 'hot' product, and neither can they vary the output. A brewer who smells that stout is selling better than lager can shift their production run within a couple of days, but a winemaker who hears that Merlot is out and Gewurztraminer is in can't exactly rip up their vines and plant new ones.

WHAT'S IN THE BOTTLE?

So what are you paying for if you buy an expensive bottle of craft beer? Partly the ingredients – you are going to get more expensive varieties of barley and more fresh hops. You are also paying much more for research and development costs – Budweiser decided on their recipe more than a hundred years ago and by and large have stuck to it, and their remaining R&D spend can be amortised across a huge output. But smaller brewers, who regularly change their recipes in order to keep up with beer enthusiasts' jaded palates, are going to be doing a lot more trial runs and throwing away a lot more failed experiments. Plus, they have much smaller production runs over which to amortise their fixed costs.

AMORTISE

1. The original sense of 'amortise' is the gradual repayment of a debt in instalments, as opposed to in one lump at the end.

2. Figuratively, based on this, any sort of 'spreading out' over time; so, in accountant speak, non-physical assets like brands and contracts are 'amortised' rather than 'depreciated'.

3. Even more figuratively, any sort of 'spreading out' at all; so one might talk about research expenditure being 'amortised' over a large production run, which would obviously be more efficient than a small one for this reason.

QUALITY CONTROL AND INDUSTRIALISATION

There is also another way in which you can be paying for beer that's thrown away at the brewery as well as the beer you drink – small brewers can have a lot more quality control issues than larger ones. This is less of a problem than it used to be with modern brewing methods, but it's still the case that industrial processes do better at large scale rather than small. In case you wish to dispute that your lovely pint represents the output from an industrial process by the way, then it might interest you to know that beer was arguably the first genuinely mass-produced product of the Industrial Revolution, and a large amount of the technical and statistical tools of standardised quality control were invented at the Guinness Brewery. However delicious and/or home-crafted your beer tipple, it undoubtedly comes from an industrial process. Otherwise it wouldn't taste so good time after time, after time, after time...

YOU ARE WHAT YOU DRINK

But realistically, can these factors, all together, come anywhere near to driving the exceptionally high retail price of craft beer? Well, they could, but they don't. We've looked through the accounts of a few small brewers and it is indeed the case that craft beer is a much higher-margin product than mass-produced beer. Not that this means that craft brewing is more profitable, or indeed profitable at all in many cases. The fixed costs are the killers here – as we say, running a scale business at small scale tends to be a labour of love rather than something that's going to make you rich.

But what you're really paying for when you buy a bottle of Steve's Flying Ricochet Ale is essentially a piece of intellectual property – in this case the brand. Above all, you're paying for a certificate of authenticity that, when you're drinking your beer, you're identifying yourself as a man (or, theoretically and in principle we suppose, a woman, but not really) of taste and discernment, and, indeed, a fellow with a few spare quid to chuck around. It is entirely possible that, if someone tried to sell craft beer cheap, then nobody would buy it.

READY FOR A ROUND-UP?

'Roundup Ready' is a brand of genetically modified maize seed that was in all the newspapers about ten years ago – it was the flagship product of Monsanto, the biotechnology company, and it attracted a lot of attention because it was the first GMO to be widely marketed and used. A lot of the protests against this product were based on general objections to the concept of genetically modified foods, and so aren't really our business in this book, but two features of Roundup Ready have quite interesting business economics and are worth a comment.

TERMINATOR
The less interesting of the two features was one of the

things that did get mentioned quite a bit during the protests – the so-called 'terminator gene'. This was a special genetic switch that meant that Roundup Ready maize plants grew inert seed rather than fertile seed. Because the seeds were inert, there was no way in which a farmer could save seedcorn from one season to plant the next – they had to buy another supply of corn from Monsanto for the next growing season. This struck a lot of people as in some way unnatural and certainly unfair.

It's actually less unfair than it looks though. Although we all have vague memories, usually rooted in long-ago-heard Bible stories, of farmers keeping their corn to plant another year, in service of some moral about thrift, almost no commercial (non-subsistence) farmers in the world actually do this. Historically, since the 'Green Revolution' in the 1960s, they have bought hybrid corn seed. Hybrid corn seeds could in principle be kept as seedcorn, and they would germinate, but this would be a really bad idea and in many ways a waste of land. Hybrid corn plants don't 'breed true' – the plants that you grew from retained seed would not have the favourable (yield, disease-resistance, taste and quality, etc.) characteristics that you had bought the hybrid seed for in the first place. Since the cost of the seed is a relatively small part of the cost of growing maize, growing from seedcorn kept back from hybrid plants would be terrible economics.

LIFE'S A BED OF MAIZE

Roundup Ready, however, wasn't like this – it was a genetically pure line, having been created by genetic engineering rather than hybridisation. So any seedcorn kept back would have bred true and grown plants that had all the nice characteristics – what characteristics? Keep reading, we'll get on to them soon. A farmer would only have had to buy it once, and they would have been in clover (well, maize) for as long as they liked.

The economics of this wouldn't have worked, for Monsanto or the farmers. If buying maize seed was a once-and-forever purchase, rather than a source of repeat business every year, then Monsanto's pricing would need to reflect this – they would need to charge not just the value of the seed, but also the value of the missed sales next year, and the year after that, and so on. This would have added up to a sum that the farmers wouldn't have been able to afford, turning the seed-purchasing process into something more akin to choosing an engagement ring or a Ming vase. Adding the 'terminator' gene to the engineering put the repeat sales back into the business model and made Roundup Ready behave like 'normal' hybridised corn, meaning that the industry didn't need to introduce a brand-new controversial product *and* a brand-new and untested business model all at the same time.

I-TERMINATOR

The terminator gene can be seen as a kind of intellectual property protection, like the Digital Rights Management code embedded into a song that you download from iTunes. In principle, it doesn't add anything to the product, but, in practice, it is the bit that makes all the rest possible. When you have a business with a marginal cost of reproduction that is very low, but an average cost (including all the infrastructure cost) that is comparatively high, then you will often see this kind of trick at work, because overheads need to be covered somehow.

READY?

But what is so special about Roundup Ready? Well, that plays into the second interesting thing about this business. Roundup Ready corn's specially engineered genetics mean that it is highly resistant to a specific kind of weedkiller – glyphosate. The most popular brand of glyphosate-based weedkiller is Roundup, also manufactured by Monsanto, hence the name: Roundup Ready corn is ready to have Roundup applied to it.

THE MAN FROM MONSANTO, HE SAY YES

In other words, the corn and the weedkiller go together, to form a 'solution' for farmers. They don't actually necessarily buy more weedkiller – the benefit of Roundup Ready corn is that you can apply your weedkiller in one large dose as the weeds come up, rather than needing to repeatedly and individually spray around each plant. But farmers who have planted Roundup Ready corn are a captive market for Roundup, and hey presto – Monsanto have managed to take two highly commoditised markets for seed and weedkiller, and put them together to get something that you might be able to make a premium profit out of.

SWEATY JANUARY – HOW GYMS MAKE MONEY

If you're a member of a gym, you will be aware that for the first month of the year the place is horribly packed out with sweaty and unfit people, all the classes are booked up and you can't get on any of the machines you want. If your interaction with the keep-fit industry is more along the lines of walking past the gym on the way to the cake shop, you might be more aware of the equally curious fact that commercial gyms always seem to have a heavily advertised 'special' membership deal going on. Paying the full whack listed rate at a gym is actually a pretty difficult thing to do – much more so than paying full freight rack-rate for a hotel room – unless you do the single most expensive thing you can do in physical culture, and join the gym shortly after the Christmas holidays.

SWEATY BETTY

Having seen the books of a gym chain or two, we can tell you that the 'Sweaty January' phenomenon is not an urban myth or a joke – it's absolutely fundamental to the economics of the industry and it's basically impossible to run an economically viable gym without taking it into account. Usually about 75 per cent of all gym memberships are taken out in the month of January. Not only this, but the economics of the industry absolutely depend on the fact that a very great proportion of January joiners will not visit more than three or four times in total before their membership comes to a floundering flop of weight not lost at the end of the year.

The founder of Colman's Mustard used to claim that his fortune was based on the bit of mustard that everyone left behind on their plate, but gym memberships have really pushed things to the limit when it comes to this model of making people pay for a lot more of the product than they have any likelihood of using.

GYM MEMBERSHIP IS FOR A YEAR, NOT JUST FOR JUST AFTER CHRISTMAS

It all starts with the subscription. There are many commercial gyms that won't let you in on a 'pay-as-you-go' basis at all, even if you beg. There are plenty of others that do, but, unless you are going to a local authority or otherwise subsidised facility, as a single-time visitor you are going to be paying the equivalent of full January prices and then some. Gym owners do not want anyone to be creating the mentality that going to the gym is something that you can pick up and put down, and enjoyed only over the beginning of the year in exactly the same way as a puppy over the Christmas period. Obviously, a lot of the people who run gyms are true believers who really want you to make a proper commitment to your own physical health and fitness, but, whether they are or not, they're subject to the same commercial pressure.

LIFE FOR RENT

And that commercial pressure is, basically, rent. A gymnasium is a high-fixed-cost business and the driver of those high fixed costs is the fact that a gym customer needs quite a bit more space compared to the retail customers in the rest of the high street, has significantly more exacting needs on the specification of that space and tends to occupy it for longer. Think about it this way:

Make a mental picture of your local supermarket, or a smallish department store or clothes shop, at a reasonably busy period. Now make another mental picture of your local gym at an equally busy period and let's start comparing them. We can note that:

1. The retail shop has more people per square foot, doesn't it, even in a snapshot? Most people tend to agree with this when we put it to them – even in the best case (for the gym owner) of row upon row of people pounding away on identical and compactly placed treadmills or exercise bikes, you just can't pack them as densely as shoppers. Very few retail customers will jig from foot to foot and wave their arms about, but people in aerobics classes do.

2. Now consider that the gym customers, unlike the customers of cafes or supermarkets, expect to be able to store their clothes while they're on the premises and to take a shower afterwards. So, for every square foot of space occupied in your mental picture of the gym, you need to allocate some changing-room space for every customer too. This probably needs to be gender-

THE SECRET LIFE OF MONEY

segregated too (most attempts to break this taboo have failed pretty disastrously), further increasing the amount of space you need.

3. Now here comes the real killer – the people in the gym are likely to be staying for at least an hour per visit, while the majority of the people in the shop will wander in, buy something and leave over a period of no more than twenty minutes. The footfall has to be measured on a per hour basis, and, on this basis, gymnasia are amazingly inefficient in terms of the usage of space.

WHEN FIXED COSTS MEET FIXED BUDGET

In terms of the fundamental equation of retailing (revenue = footfall x purchases per visit x average ticket size – see page 75), gyms have pretty lousy footfall built into the business model, but excellent conversion percentage; more or less by definition, everyone occupying the space is paying to do so and thereby making a purchase. But they are so inefficient in terms of generating the customer turnover that it's really difficult to make the fixed cost economics work, because the amount you'd need to charge per 'sale' would end up being beyond the means of most of the users.

Unless ... unless you could push the conversion rate much higher than 100 per cent, by having people paying for the gymnasium services while not actually using them. Hence, Sweaty January. Here you have customers paying upfront, but turning up only once, twice, perhaps four times in total during the year. They then either, realistically, conclude that they have given enough free money to the gym, that gym membership is not for them, and don't renew. Or the gym owner's dream, they repeat to fade every year – joining each January with good intentions, and never turning up beyond each mid-March, until expanding waistlines and increasing guilt hold sway each coming Christmas time and they renew.

The moral of the story is either use it or lose it – the membership that is. Or, if you're planning to have a short burst of good intentions, make sure you do it in midsummer when gyms are desperate for new members and will slash prices accordingly.

SECURITY THROUGH
MATURITY

'Security through maturity' is one of those useful little phrases that you can drop into any semi-related conversation in order to plant the fear in people's minds that you might know what you're talking about. It's a bit of jargon (as is 'seniority by priority', which means the same thing and is useful for dropping into conversations when someone else has already done 'security through maturity'), but it's pretty straightforward to unpack. However, it does refer to some fairly subtle and advanced concepts, which even industry veterans often fail to keep straight, sometimes at a cost of considerable amounts of money and embarrassment. You might want to drop this phrase when you, or your organisation, are owed money, and you are worried about getting it back. So it's originally a banker's phrase, but, if you're a supplier to another company (or a professional services business – law firms are famous for tolerating the most absurd delays between doing the work and collecting the money), you can also end up in one of those huddled meetings where everyone gets a little bit worried about whether the accounts receivable are ever going to turn into accounts paid.

So, let's unpack the phrase. First, 'security'. Effectively, if a firm is going bust, then it's likely that some creditors will get paid and some won't. Obviously, you want to be one of the ones that will. Clearly, one of the best ways to achieve that would be to walk into the debtor company's factory, carry off something valuable, and sell it to offset your debt. We are not endorsing this action, obviously. Apart from anything else, if everyone did that, it would result in an undignified squabble that would massively reduce the overall value of the firm, and ensure that the total loss was a lot bigger than it might have been had the debtor been wound up in a sensible and orderly fashion.

THE PECKING ORDER

So there are legal arrangements governing the ability of creditors to do this. Top of the tree comes a 'fixed charge holder'. This is someone whose loan agreement specifically provides that they can take possession of a specific asset, usually a building. That's about as secure as you can be, since usually the asset will be worth a lot more than the loan it's secured on (in which case, the excess sale proceeds go back to the remaining creditors once the fixed charge holder has been paid in full). Next down the ladder you have 'floating charge holders', who have a charge on all the assets, whatever they might be, which don't have specific charges on them from somebody else. Once they have been given enough assets to pay themselves in full, everybody else gets paid from whatever is left, and, if that's not enough to pay them all back, they take a loss.

(For the purpose of that simplified example, we're only talking about the normal kind of creditors. There are lots of special kinds, like the taxman, unpaid wages and so on, who have a particular place in the pecking order specified in legislation. The most senior creditor of all, getting paid immediately after the fixed charge holders, are the guys who administrate the wind-up. It's worth learning the full list, but it varies a bit by legal jurisdiction. One thing worth knowing, though, is that, in most of the world, unpaid bills to suppliers tend to be right down there with the unsecured creditors – you can't presume that you're going to be able to repossess the tray of widgets you supplied.)

SENIORITY BY PRIORITY

So, if you're down the pecking order, how do you improve your position? Well, basically, the best way to make sure that you get paid is to *get paid*. That's the concept of 'security by maturity' in a nutshell. If the floating charge holder is a bank loan that matures in ten years' time and your bill is due today, then there's a strong sense in which you are the senior creditor – because you get paid and then make a decision about whether you want to supply any more thirty-day terms to the borrower, while the bank loan can't be revisited for ten years.

DON'T LET BYGONES BE BYGONES

If this seems too good to be true, that's because often it is. The bankruptcy trustee is usually allowed to 'look back' and 'claw back' payments of an insolvent company, with a look-back period that can be as much as two years, forcing creditors who have been paid to return the payments so that there is more to be divided up in the bankruptcy. The idea is to make things a bit fairer (so that the division of pain is not determined simply on the basis of who happened to have a bill due two days before rather than two days after), to encourage longer-term lending (by removing the incentive to scramble for security by maturity), and to cut out a lot of the desperate

– and often counterproductive – behaviour indulged in by directors of nearly bankrupt companies, who try to play creditors off one against another to buy time in the hope that a miracle will turn up.

IN PRACTICE...

Having said that, insolvency practitioners are by nature a practical lot. They know that chasing up clawbacks is a time-consuming and expensive business, and in a lot of cases more trouble than it's worth. For one thing, if they run up more costs in trying to chase up clawbacks than they actually get, they have failed to do their job and might get sued by the unsecured creditors. And for another, they are well aware that seriously burning the trade creditors is usually a bad idea if you are trying to sell the thing as a going concern, which is what they want to do most of all. So, although, in principle, the law provides for clawbacks, in practice, and particularly for small bills, security by maturity works better than you'd expect. This is one more reason to not allow those accounts receivable to fester for longer than you can possibly help.

GETTING PAID ON GOVERNMENT DEBT

The case in which security by maturity really, really matters is in *sovereign* lending. When countries borrow on the international markets, there is essentially no bankruptcy law and no possibility of clawback, so possession of the cash is ten-tenths of the law. People who bought the Greek government bonds that matured in March 2012 got paid in full; people who bought the bonds that matured in November 2012 lost 70 per cent of their money. That's why the biggest danger sign you can see for sovereign debt in a developing country is a rapid shortening of the average debt term. Not only does this make the borrowing cost much more volatile, as it is driven by shorter-term interest rates, but, once the average maturity has shortened, it is the devil's own job for the sovereign to lengthen it again, because all the bond investors know that to extend a longer maturity is to effectively accept that you are going to get paid last, should anything bad happen.

TV FORMATS AND BRANDS
OR, YOU ARE THE WEAKEST LINK.
GOODBYE

When you think about it, the fortune of Simon Cowell is based on two massive successes – *American Idol* and America's *The X Factor*. Or, to put it bluntly, 'selling the Americans the right to host a talent show for themselves' and 'selling the Americans the right to host a talent show for themselves, again'. It pretty much defines the phrase 'nice work if you can get it'. What is going on here?

Like newspaper mastheads, brands or other recognisable creative works, a TV show format can be copyrighted and licensed. But the licensing and branding has to refer to a quite tightly defined format; you can't just claim blanket ownership of the entire concept of 'a competition for kids trying to get a record contract'. So, on the face of it, it seems like there might be a bit of a puzzle as to why international stations would be falling over themselves to pay to use licensed formats. And this is big business: it is in large measure due to these two shows that Simon Cowell's fortune stands at an estimated £425m. To take another example, *Strictly Come Dancing* is quite possibly as big an export earner for the UK as the whole steel industry.

BUY NOT BUILD

The reason why people seem to buy these formats is the same reason why big firms buy up smaller competitors (particularly in the web industry) rather than building their own copycat version. And that is, in an uncertain world where nobody has the formula for success and failures are really expensive, there are few things quite as attractive as a functioning prototype. Indeed, even in the world of physical and mechanical inventions, a lot of intellectual property lawyers will tell you that, rather than going through the laborious and expensive business of getting your new widget patented, you're better off taking it to an existing firm in the widget industry and getting them to buy your trade secrets. Because, in many cases, the best intellectual property protection in the world is being able to say, 'I know *exactly* how to do this, and I can prove that, if you do it my way, it works, and it will take you a lot more time and effort to work that out for yourself than to pay me.' What a format licence buys you, as well as the branding, is the 'bible' – the thick three-ring binder detailing absolutely every detail of how the original production was put together.

HAVING THE 'X' FACTOR
This is how TV formats work. Like them or loathe them, the big-ticket Cowell formats are proven hits in country after country. And because of them, or in spite of them, the Johnny-come-lately knock-off versions rolled out by competing broadcasters have a track record of ignominious flopping – remember *Fame Academy*? Getting even something as simple as a competition to find the valuable antiques in a junk shop is actually a pretty skilled and finely balanced affair, and, if you're tweaking the format sufficiently to be able to claim it's not a straightforward rip-off of the concept, you're very likely to have tweaked it so much that the magic no longer works. That's why TV game-show formats are among the very rare pieces of globally traded intellectual property.

VALUING BRANDS

These days, valuing brands is a substantial industry in itself. There are a number of consultancies – some of them really rather big – that will give you a precise number, in dollars and cents, of how much a brand is worth (although the stockbroker among the authors notes that they don't actually stand ready to buy or sell at that price…). Interbrand even publishes a league table on a yearly basis of the world's most valuable brands. All of which raises a number of questions, the first and most important one being – what the hell are these people going on about?

THE GAZETTE AND GOODWILL

Right, think of an imaginary town, Exampleville, with its town newspaper, called the *Exampleville Gazette*. It has a good name and reputation, plus strong relationships with advertisers and a subscriber list. If the value of the typewriters and printing presses is $1000, then you're clearly not going to be able to buy this business for that price alone. You'll have to pay some bigger number, which we will call $X.

The difference between $X and the $1000 value of the physical assets is called the *goodwill*. It's the intangible asset reflecting the value added to those assets by putting them together in the context of a business. Goodwill shows up all the time in accountancy, because companies are always buying things from each other, and rarely purely for the depreciated value of the physical stuff.

SIGN OF THE TIMES

So is goodwill the value of the brand? Nope. There are a lot of things contributing to that asset other than the good name and reputation of the *Exampleville Gazette*. The subscriber list is worth something. The advertiser relationships too. What you want to know is the value that's purely attributable to the brand. So, if you would be prepared to pay $X for the *Gazette* as a whole, but only $Y if the owner stipulated that you weren't allowed to call it the *Exampleville Gazette* any more, then the difference between X and Y would be the pure value of the brand.

We've chosen the example of a newspaper because, historically, newspaper companies used to be just about the only companies that recorded the value of their brands in their company accounts. And the reason for that is that newspaper mastheads were more or less the only pieces of branded property that were regularly traded between buyers and sellers, but *without* selling the associated business. That would happen in this way. Imagine another newspaper in town, say the *Exampleville Times*. It was an OK business, but not as good as the *Gazette*. It wasn't uncommon for the owner of the *Times* to just pay the owner of the *Gazette* for the right to the name!

If that's a bit difficult to get your head round, imagine you've just written a novel about scheming lawyers; you might consider it money well spent to pay John Grisham some amount to persuade him to let you put his name on the cover rather than, or as well as, yours. This has never actually happened in the specific case of Grisham, but similar transactions do go on all the time – look for novels co-authored by Tom Clancy and Someone Else and note the size of the typefaces of the two names! The sum of money you had to pay Famous Author for their name on your book is clearly the traded value, at that moment, of their brand.

PINNING DOWN THE VALUE

If you're not in the habit of doing open market deals for brands, it's very tough to value them, because it's much less clear how much of the value is attributable specifically to the brand name, and how much to all the other things that go into the business of making the product. In fact, a lot of people would still say, if you pushed them, that it's basically impossible in most cases, and that the brand is inseparable from all the other goodwill and intangible assets. Basically, if you find an accountant over forty-five years of age and pour half a bottle of wine down his neck, he will usually admit that brand assets are a load of baloney.

FREE LOVE ON THE FREE LOVE FREEWAY (OR THE BALANCE SHEET)

However, there are often purposes for which it's useful to have a value of a brand in your balance sheet – if you're fighting off a takeover attempt and want to write down a number for the company's assets that is as high as possible, for example. Or less controversially, if you're a company in a branded goods market that's often in the habit of doing takeovers yourself, and wants to treat brands that you developed internally on a reasonably consistent basis with brands that you acquired as the result of corporate deals (which would have had goodwill payments associated with them). And this is quite possible now since there are plenty of younger and less fuddy-duddy accountants who don't have a problem with long hair, free love and internally generated goodwill on the balance sheet.

If you want to value a brand, you have to make a

discounted cash flow (DCF) model (see your favourite business school textbook – if you don't have one, then mentally substitute 'a magic spreadsheet that gives you a usually rather spurious but toothsomely precise number for the financial value of a company or project'). Yes, I know – such fun! Basically, you model the business as it is, then you estimate what its sales and margins would be if it didn't have the brand, and model it again. The difference between the two valuations is the value attributable to the brand. Sounds rigorous, huh?

Err, yeah ... If you have ever done one yourself, you'll know that it's a poor analyst who can't get whatever answer they want out of a DCF model, and this is even more so when you've got so many totally subjective inputs to the model – not only are you able to play around with overhead cost allocations, discount rates and all the other tools of the experienced DCF fiddler, but the most important input to the whole shooting match is the 'brand premium' and that is a number that, subject to the loosest of constraints of common sense and good practice, you can pluck out of the air.

BOTTOM OF THE LEAGUE

This is one of the reasons why consultancies like Interbrand are so keen on making league tables of 'The

World's Most Valuable Brands'. It's mostly a marketing exercise for their consultancy and valuation services, of course it is. But it's also the case that a league table of some sort is basically the only check at all on the modelling flexibility – if you've managed to value the Dell brand higher than Apple, or Panda Cola higher than Coca-Cola, then you know that you've done something wrong. If you've got a large spread of brand valuations in your files, though, and there's a reasonable consensus about the rough ordering of them in terms of which is more valuable than which, then you've got a reasonable cross check on the DCF methodology.

SHHHH!

Top Secret – we gave you the official methodology for valuing brands there, the one that's written into the relevant accounting standard. In actual fact, everyone just looks into their files of 'industry comparables', then fiddles the DCF to be roughly consistent, updating the files as a whole periodically to make sure that the 'brand value' is a reasonably constant proportion of the market capitalisation.

Don't tell the auditors we said that.

BIG TICKETS FOR BIG TICKETS – MONEY BROKERS

Have you ever thought, when the newspapers report that front-row seats for the latest Madonna concert are selling for $500 each, *Who on earth pays that kind of money for these things?* The answer is, very often, 'Money brokers, entertaining their clients'.

TAX AND SPEND
Money brokers – dealers in short-dated loans, foreign exchange and interest rate derivatives – spend more money on client entertainment than nearly any other industry in the world. This actually has financial implications for assessing the sturdiness or otherwise of a money brokerage – when you're analysing a money-

broking company, you have to bear in mind that a very large proportion of their expenses are not allowable by the income tax. (In the UK at least, the taxman takes a somewhat puritanical attitude to wining and dining on the company tab – entertainment expenses are not deductible.) For this reason, money brokers often find themselves paying corporation tax rates up to 50 per cent or even higher on their actual economic profits.

COMMODITY SPIRIT

Why do they spend so much? The essential answer is because they are a completely commoditised business. There's almost no differentiation whatsoever between the products that each of them offers – literally, anyone's money is as good as anyone else's. Every now and then, there will be a technological leap forward in the industry and somebody will capture a load of market share with a new electronic trading platform, or by offering a new contract that makes it more convenient to trade a particular bundle of financial instruments. But there's virtually no intellectual property in the industry because it's very difficult to patent a financial idea, so any of these innovations are quickly copied across the industry.

PARTY HARDY

Which means that there are only two ways for a money-broker business to get work – either happen to be the guy or gal on the other end of the telephone (or electronic equivalent) when one of the big clients wants to make a trade, or persuade the clients to give you the business, because you're one of their mates. Which means pop concerts, sports events and (because the global money-broking industry is mainly centred on London rather than the more abstemious and/or 'professional' financial centres) alcohol. Lots and lots of alcohol. Money brokers are notorious in the City of London for being the most full-on party animals, and most of the most famous stories of drunken (and yeah, coked-up) behaviour are attributable to this corner of the street.

In general, we would advise against socialising with money brokers unless you have first equipped yourself with a cast-iron excuse for chipping and running at a very early stage in the evening. However much of an iron liver you think you have, money brokers are worse.

JOLLIES FOR THE BOYS

It kind of sounds here as if the money-broking industry is a pretty valueless chiz – a big 24/7 jolly carried out at the expense of the shareholders in the clients' companies, who might benefit from somewhat lower costs of lending and borrowing in the short-term deposits market if they did their trading face to face, without the 'help' of the guys with the Madonna tickets. On the face of it, this looks like a rather corrupt old boys' (generally not girls') network.

MALCOLM IN THE MIDDLE

Is it? Well ... not totally. We are certainly not going to stand up for every single practice of the money-broking industry, and the fact that the business has shrunk massively over the last two decades (consolidated down to only two or three players, who nowadays seem to spend half their time poaching staff from one another, and the other half in pointless lawsuits over poaching staff from each other – since it's a game of relationships, I don't think we need a whole chapter to explain why this happens) does suggest it was a rather bloated sector. But the money brokers, or, to give them an alternative title that provides something more of a clue as to their function, the 'inter-dealer brokers', do have a function in the market. And that function is quite simple – *they are middlemen.*

GOING DOWN?

Put yourself in the shoes of a trader at a large bank or insurance company who has got a big order to fill. What's the one thing that you don't want anyone to know? *That you've got a big order to fill.* Because a big order is going to require several trades in order to get the thing executed. And if people notice that it's always you out in the market selling, say, two-year French government bonds, then they're going to guess that the reason you're always there and you're always selling is because you've got a very big order to shift. And what do you do if you're a trader who finds out or guesses that there's a big sell order out in the market? Sell a few yourself, because you know that the big order is going to drive the price down.

Insider dealing – trading a security because you have secret knowledge that something nasty, or nice, is going to happen to it – is illegal. But *deducing* that something nasty is going to happen to a particular security, by looking at the order flow and noticing that it's always the same person and they're always selling, is the opposite of illegal. It's the definition of what it is to be a good trader. When there's a rogue trader scandal on the evening news – a Nick Leeson or a Jerome Kerviel – then the traders in the relevant markets have a big party. They know that the bank that's discovered the rogue trader is going to have to unwind a big position over the next few days, and that's the best kind of news that you can get, because you know which way to bet on price movements, and make some more or less certain money.

TELL IT TO THE JUDGE

This fact often comes up in the trials of the rogues, incidentally – their defence lawyers often argue that the telephone-number losses that their employers have sustained are mainly a result of the publicity and the poor handling of the unwind of the position. This defence strategy, while potentially economically valid, doesn't usually let the defendants off the hook. Jerome Kerviel still owes his former employer, Societe Generale, somewhere in the region of $880m. Few people think that SG is ever going to get that money back; the bank has said that for the meantime they're not inclined to pursue it, and a lot of us think that what they really want to do is make sure that he doesn't have any economic incentive to write a book. He will just have to do it for the love of it then, like us.

Anyway, returning to money brokers. Given all the nasty things that can happen to you if the world finds out that you're trying to execute a big order, rather than just trading lots of little ones, wouldn't it be great if there was something you could do to anonymise yourself?

Like, say, to give the order to a third party who would then go out on your behalf to find a Buy to match your Sell, without giving up your identity? And if this third party had enough two-way business going over their books that it would be much more difficult for anyone observing their transaction pattern to deduce anything about the larger orders in the market, wouldn't that help? That's the service that money brokers provide.

WHO'S IN THE KNOW?

The difference between *informed* and *uninformed* buying and selling is always absolutely crucial in financial markets. But it matters in quite a lot of other markets, too. Outlet malls often get a surprisingly good mix of active and current lines from their fashion suppliers, simply because the suppliers don't want people to be always able to work out when they're dumping an overstock of a line that didn't sell. Art dealers have all sorts of Byzantine practices (of the sort you can get away with in a more or less completely unregulated market) with respect to the identities of buyers and sellers. Even in used-car markets, we would all like to know whether the previous owner of this Focus was a nineteen-year-old boy racer or the proverbial little old lady. In a lot of markets, the identity of the traders is valuable information, and so it shouldn't be surprising that, in a lot of industries, the management of that valuable information is itself a service that middlemen are paid money for.

KICKING BACK THE WHISKY

But, although middlemen are useful, they're only a little bit useful. And since the service they provide is just simply one of being in the right place at the right time, a middleman business (a wholesaler, auction house, etc.) can never get really fantastic operating margins. In fact, well-managed middleman businesses – and this fact is a staple of analysis of the money-broking and stock exchange sector – will often regard an operating margin that is too high in their business as being every bit as dangerous a surprise as one which is too low. When you're running a business like a money broker, you can't be seen to be making massive profits, or your customers will start looking around to find a cheaper way of producing the anonymity you provide – and it's awfully difficult to turn anonymity into a branded good.

So any improvements in technology, business practices and general efficiency tend to get kicked back to the customers. In the long term, in the form of structurally reducing margins; in the short term, in the form of front-row seats and expensive Scotch whiskies.

THE SECRET WEAPON OF
MARTIAL ARTS SCHOOLS

The story is familiar to every town in the country. You decide you want to take up a martial art so you check out the various schools in your area. They have wildly different names and each claim a distinctive lineage stretching back into Shaolin history, yet when you speak to them and visit them they look and feel the same, teaching exactly the same style of martial arts. So why do they claim such different origins? The answer is that they are not so much competing schools of martial arts as ... competing insurance brokers. Insurance is the secret weapon that martial arts schools use in their fight for profits.

The business of running a martial arts school is pretty much the same as running any other kind of gym (see

Sweaty January); you sign up as many people as possible with an upfront fee, and hope that most of them give up pretty quickly. But martial arts schools are a little bit different from other kinds of gym in two ways. First, they have more than the normal demand for personal injury insurance, and, second, the highest grades of any martial art are the instructor grades. As a result, schools tend to regularly produce individuals who want to open up their own martial arts clubs, as each school can only have a few teachers actually working there. This is what gives them their own distinctive and rather interesting business economics.

MARTIAL ARTS: THE WAY OF THE INSURANCE BROKER

In general, martial arts schools insure through the Lloyd's of London market, via a small number of syndicates who specialise in providing professional indemnity insurance to people engaging in dangerous sports. If you've ever met a representative sample of insurance underwriters (try hanging around the wine bars on Cornhill in London if this is really your aim, although we don't accept any liability, personal or otherwise, for the consequences), you'll appreciate that, for the most part, they're not the kind of people who have any first-hand ability to judge the riskiness or competence of any kind of athletic pursuit. And so, when they're writing insurance on this sort of thing, they tend to look around for anything that looks like a nice 'official'-looking organisation, headed by acknowledged experts in the field.

And so, when Fred 'Blue Dragon' Bloggs wants to start up his new kung fu class in the village hall of Brinkley, near Redditch, he buys the personal accident insurance he needs for him and his intrepid students via a middleman, such as the Yie Ar Wing Chun Association of Great Britain, which will usually consist of a wise old Chinese man with a genuine martial arts pedigree, plus one of his relatives who knows a bit about insurance and the Lloyd's market. Fred is then a qualified Sifu in Yie Ar Wing Chun, until he concludes that he's paying over the odds for his insurance, at which point he will have a spiritual and martial epiphany, and his martial arts club will start along the path of Ving Gau Ba Gua Tai Chi; in other words, the same bunch of punch/chop/kick guys, but they happen to be charging a bit less at the time for their insurance contracts. If you read the classified advertisements at the back of *Fighting Arts International*, *Black Belt* or similar monthly martial arts magazines, you will see these different 'schools' advertised to instructors in commendably straightforward and honest commercial terms.

PASS GO, COLLECT £200

But what happens when Fred Blue Dragon finds that one of his Grasshoppers is ready to hop off on his own? In general, the Yie Ar Wing Chun Association of Great Britain will not certify another instructor to 'teach' their 'style' (i.e. to be insured via them) within a certain geographical radius of an existing school. If you read their marketing literature, this is out of respect for the relationship between the Master and his disciples, the preservation of the local traditions, blah, blah, blah. In actual fact, it is a pretty cheap and easy way of sustaining a number of little regional monopolies – if Yie Ar Wing Chun were to explicitly say that they were refusing to allow two martial arts schools to compete in the same town in order to stop them from cutting prices against one another, eventually the Trading Standards people would get interested. However, if you're in the business of certifying people for an insurance liability, then you will typically find that no non-expert outsider will gainsay your decisions, not with a ten-foot pole, and expert *insiders* will typically be very reluctant to tell tales on one another – quite apart from anything else, given this is the martial arts field, there is always the risk of getting your head kicked in.

Which is another reason for the proliferation of seemingly identical but subtly different 'styles' of martial arts – it's often the only way that a newly minted black belt wanting to earn some proper money as a personal trainer can get a look in.

WHAT'S IN A TRADEMARK?

To take things a little further, these various styles are aggressively trademarked: if you want to see a really bitterly fought-out intellectual property case, have a look at some of the American court dockets related to 'jiu-jitsu'. This is the Portuguese spelling of the Japanese word 'ju-jitsu'. (Fun fact: there was huge Japanese emigration to Brazil at the end of the nineteenth century, as a result of a few real estate developers who successfully marketed it as the New World.) In the early 1990s, a couple of jiu-jitsu wrestlers, members of the extremely prolific and quite frighteningly hard Gracie family, absolutely cleaned up in the Ultimate Fighting Championships. As a result, 'jiu-jitsu', so branded, became massively popular and lucrative in the USA – as a martial art, it is really like the judo that they used to teach down your local sports centre, with the crucial difference that it costs twenty quid per class more. And, as a result of *that*, various branches of the Gracie family, their mates and their hangers-on became involved in vast amounts of trademark litigation on the general subject of what was and wasn't 'jiu-jitsu', who was and wasn't a Gracie, and so on.

The obvious solution to these questions – that is, leaving the lawyers out of it and just settling everything with a fight – was actually tried on a couple of occasions, which goes to show that there are easy and difficult ways of earning a living.

WHAT DO AIR MILES HAVE IN COMMON WITH THE ZIMBABWEAN DOLLAR?

Air miles were launched in America thirty years ago as a loyalty scheme by American Airlines. It was simply a new marketing wheeze to get people to take more flights with the airline more often. The scheme grew and grew, and now includes 130 airlines in the world, with air miles being collected from shopping, credit card spending, etc. as well as flying, and with the resulting free flights enjoyed to Paris, Timbuktu – and even space – being the talk of many a dinner party.

FREE FLIGHT TO SPACE

Alan Watts from Harrow had saved two million air miles with Virgin Atlantic by repeatedly flying upper class to America, and in 2006 he was contacted by Virgin Galactic to ask if he would like to spend them on a 2½-hour flight into space (although this sounds very Hitchhiker's Guide, we are genuinely not making this up). Alan understandably assumed it was a prank call, but Virgin were apparently serious, and Mr Watts will fly into space as soon as Virgin Galactic begin flights, although no one quite knows when that will be...

BUT THERE IS A PROBLEM...

The problem is that more air miles have been issued than could ever be redeemed. It has been estimated that there are over $2 trillion worth of air miles in circulation and it is growing by 20 per cent each year. To put this in perspective, this is more than the total value of US dollars in global circulation. Indeed, it is around a fifth of the global money supply for all currencies in the world, which is estimated at $10.5 trillion.

This has not gone unnoticed by the airlines, who have wisely reacted to prevent total currency meltdown.

While some commentators in recent years have predicted that air miles would have to announce currency reform – such as when the Mark in Germany in 1923 was re-floated as the Rentenmark at a rate of one-billionth of the Mark's value – the airlines themselves have preferred a salami slice approach. So, as every year passes and the number of air miles grows ever more unsustainably, so the number of restrictions on how they can be used also grows, and the exchange rate at which they can be traded shrinks.

When air miles were launched, one air mile earned was directly exchangeable for one air mile that could be flown, with a particular airline, but to any destination, at any time. These days, air miles can only be spent to particular destinations, at particular (for which read unpopular) times, and sometimes only with the customer committing to further tied expenses, such as booking a hotel or car hire through the airline. As Nazmeera Moola, head of Macro strategy at Macquarie First South, has observed: 'If you can't spend the miles, then the value of the outstanding miles is a fair bit less than US$1 trillion. Air miles are probably the most overvalued currency in the world.'

The comparison with the hyperinflated Zimbabwean dollar is almost perfect, except that people in Zimbabwe realise that their currency is near worthless, but most people don't seem to realise that their air miles are becoming so.

SO WHAT SHOULD WE DO ABOUT IT?

Spend 'em! The old philosophy that one could amass air miles through a business career working and then spend them in retirement on trips around the world is almost certainly a thing of the past, and certainly shouldn't be relied on as an integral part of your pension. Air miles are not to be saved any longer, otherwise you might find you have saved a whole heap of nothing. Out with prudence, in with profligacy!

WHEN IS £50 WORTH MORE THAN £50?

If you have the right sort of friends (and evidently we don't), you may be personally aware that Liberty, the shop in London, produces beautiful embossed £50 'coins', which can be bought for, er, £50 and then given as gifts for people to spend in the Liberty shop. (Not in any other shops: that would be something like real liberty.) So this is just a classic gift certificate scheme, like the book tokens of old, I hear you cry; what makes this any different? The difference is that Liberty has had a cunning plan: to turn the token into a beautiful object, a thing that people will want to keep on their mantelpieces rather than exchange for half a water-damaged floral notebook, or whatever you can buy for £50 in Liberty.

THE SECRET LIFE OF MONEY

A TOKEN GIFT

In the old token system, someone pays Liberty £50 for a piece of paper, which their friend then exchanges for some goods in Liberty that cost around £50, giving Liberty whatever profit they usually make on their goods (generally around 10 per cent, e.g. £5). They might make a little more out of the trade of course, because the token and its non-tradability in other shops might make the gift receiver go to Liberty when they might not otherwise have done, and it also might make them buy something more expensive than £50 and use the token as part payment. So this sounds like a pretty good deal for Liberty.

LIBERTY HALL

But compare it with the shiny penny trade: in this case, someone has given Liberty £50 in exchange for a pretty coin and box, which probably cost Liberty about £2 to make. The friend then keeps this coin forever and Liberty keeps the cash, in this case £48. Even if the friend does eventually spend it, any inflation will mean that they get less for the £50 in the future than they would have done at the time of the present being received. Indeed, even if there is little or no inflation, Liberty will still have had the cash to invest, or spend on sweets, until such time as the gift receiver does pull their finger out and choose something from the shop.

GOLF AS CURRENCY

For the British Open of 2005, the Royal Bank of Scotland (which like the Bank of England and two other Scottish banks, for various historic reasons, has rights to issue money) issued commemorative banknotes with Jack Nicklaus' face on them. The Open, which was sponsored by RBS, was also persuaded by them to stock their tills exclusively with the Nicklaus pounds. They were real money, not 'Itchy and Scratchy money' of *Simpsons* fame – this was sold in Itchy and Scratchyland and marketed as 'like normal money but more fun' but actually was found to be accepted almost nowhere, just after Homer had converted $1,100 into the stuff.

The Nicklaus money was real money and so could be traded anywhere in Scotland, or indeed theoretically in England or Wales (but some shops do look at you funny if you try to exchange a Scottish 'poond' for English goods to the value of an English pound). There are no Welsh pounds. But the genius of the scheme, from RBS's point of view, was that RBS rightly banked on people not wanting to exchange their Nickpounds for goods or services, but instead to keep them on their mantelpieces of sporting homage. The result is pure profit for the bank (and also a slight implication for the money supply, which the Bank of England might have something to say about, but we won't go into that now).

It is estimated that all of the 2 million £5 notes issued (a total of £10 million) are still hanging around homes and golf clubs in the country not being spent.

PENNY BLACK
And don't get us onto the subject of stamp collectors, the Royal Mail's favourite customers: if you buy a stamp and never exchange it for postal services, you've paid roughly 2000 times the cost of producing a very small piece of sticky paper...

SPEND, SPEND!
The moral here is the same as with the air-miles moral (see page 195): spend, spend, spend! Yes, the shiny penny is nice but it is evidently not in fact worth the £50 printed on its face. If you like pretty coins, then go and get some from an old coin shop. Moreover, any time you waste in not spending the 'money' is time that Liberty or whoever is the issuer has the money, not you. Unless you have a plan to wait for the sales, spend and spend now.

In the golfing example, of course, the money *is* worth what it says on its face, but it's not earning any interest while it's just sitting in your desk drawer. There are three possible solutions here: either you don't trust banks so all your money is under the mattress in which case this can just join the rest, but should still be considered fair game to be spent come a rainy day. Or spend it when you would all the rest of your money, and just don't look it in the face when doing so. Or don't be such a sucker for sporting heroes in the first place.

SYMPATHY FOR THE INSURANCE COMPANY DEVIL

The insurance industry is one of the ones that it is often tempting to leave for the specialists to understand, because it's very techy and in many ways very boring. Leaving it to the specialists is often the right thing to do, if you have someone at hand who knows their stuff and whom you trust. But, if you don't (or since you may not at some important future date), it's worth knowing enough about the way insurance works to be at least a little streetwise. There's no point in giving a comprehensive list of the tricks that insurance contracts can contain, not least because they're always inventing new ones. But here we can take our usual approach of giving a few examples of the *kinds* of tricks that go on, in the hope that you'll pick up the general principles and figure out where to look yourself.

INSURANCE HEAVEN

Let's start with the basics. How do insurance companies make their money? Surely it's from the difference between the money we give them in premiums and the money they pay out in claims. Right?

Wrong. It's a nice idea, and insurance companies would certainly like to do this, but it's not actually the bread and butter of where their money comes from. In insurance heaven, they make their profit by careful underwriting: i.e. they work out the price of a whole bunch of risks added together given the average scenario that my house gets broken into but your house doesn't. Then they add a bit more to make sure they don't go bust when there's a hurricane, or in case they've underestimated how much crime there's going to be. Then they add on a bit more to cover their costs, and a bit more than that to make a profit.

That's insurance heaven. But most insurance companies live in insurance hell. Here's why: insurance companies need to be big to make money. And this means fierce competition by other firms looking to increase their market share.

WHY ARE THERE NO SMALL 'MOM AND POP' INSURANCE COMPANIES?

Insurance companies come in three sizes; quite big, very big and massive. It is in fact not legal to start one up unless you can show that you're able to run it on a sufficient scale. Why? Because big risk pools are more efficient than little ones. Think about it this way; pretend that a car costs £10,000, and every car has a 1 per cent chance of crashing in a year. The 'fair' premium is therefore £100.

If you are insuring only one car, then your claims are always going to be either £0 or £10,000. Therefore, you need to keep £10,000 of cash on hand to pay out claims. If you're only making £100 of premiums, your return on capital is 1 per cent, which is almost certainly not enough to cover your costs.

If, on the other hand, you are insuring 1 million cars, then your claims are very likely indeed to be close to 1 per cent x 1,000,000 x £10,000 = £100 million (10,000 cars crashing at £10,000 a car). But your premiums are also going to be £100 million (1 million premiums at £100/car). If you keep enough cash around to make sure you can still pay claims if the actual claim rate turns out to be five times as much as expected (£500m), then you're still making a 20 per cent return on your capital.

This is the 'Law of Large Numbers', and it is the

basis of insurance. Basically, the larger the risk pool, the more likely that the actual outcome will be close to its expected value. In case you're wondering how specialist insurance operations (like the ones that insure martial arts schools or supermodels' legs) get off the ground, the answer is that they are usually actually insurance 'brokers', rather than underwriters – they assess the risk and set the premium, but then sell the insurance contract on to a bigger firm, via the Lloyd's market or similar. This is known as 'reinsurance'.

INSURANCE HELL

Apart from the constant quest for market share in the insurance industry in order to take advantage of the law of large numbers, the second reason it is difficult to run an insurance company at an underwriting profit is a little more obscure and drives a load of behaviour in the industry, ranging from 'interesting' to 'pathological'. It's basically this: you as the insurer are aiming to get information on the average payout on the average risk. But each one of your customers is trying to insure their own specific risk. And while these risks are (presumably) all sufficiently similar to each other to be pooled together, they're not exactly all the same. So who do you think knows most about each individual risk: you, the insurer, or your customer? Potentially the customer.

NOT THE AVERAGE

Your insurance exposure isn't to the average of all the risks out there – it's an exposure to a group of people who thought that buying insurance at the rate you were offering it was a good deal for them. A good deal for them doesn't necessarily mean a bad deal for you, because insurance can be a win-win situation. But it does mean that you need to be cautious that you haven't picked up an 'adverse selection'.

A LITTLE KNOWLEDGE

Lots of insurance industry funniness stems from this. It's the reason why policies have an excess on them; making the customer share some of the risk tends to calm down the incentive to profit from their information advantage over the insurer. But it also encourages insurance companies to look for situations and markets in which they can get their information advantage back. In particular, it's one of the reasons why insurance companies love to have bells and whistles on their policies, which make direct comparison of the price and coverage difficult. The last thing they want to deal with is an informed customer.

A BROAD SPECTRUM

It also means that insurance companies, since they know that informed customers can be dangerous, have a tendency to try to get absolutely as much profitability as they can out of the other kind. The difference between the cheapest and most expensive quote for some insurance products can be absolutely massive, even though the difference in coverage can be tiny. Having sold a policy on the cheap with a large excess, the insurer might take a punt that it can get some of the margin back by selling the customer a policy to 'insure the excess' for literally ten times what it's worth. What they are doing here is betting the customer won't spot that the potential loss the company is insuring on the original policy could go very high indeed, but the excess amount is by definition limited.

Equally, notoriously, the providers of extended warranties will take advantage of the fact that it's difficult to estimate the reliability of consumer durables or the cost of repairs. And so on.

CHEAP AND NASTY

Because there's an advantage to being big, there's usually someone in the insurance market who is prepared to cut prices in order to increase their presence in the market. And unfortunately, it's perfectly possible for them to set a price below the 'fair' premium (the premium that reflects the actual loss rate) and still stay in business. How come? Because the nature of insurance business is that you get the premium upfront, and pay the claims later, when they arise. Insurance companies are therefore able to earn interest on the 'float' – the cash they get upfront – while they are waiting for a claim to happen. Investment return is therefore a key part of the profit of an insurance company.

A RAINY DAY

Making money on investment is fine when the economy is doing well, but it leaves insurance companies very exposed in a recession, when investment income usually falls. And that's not the only reason that insurance companies deserve our sympathy. As a business model, the industry has several other fatal flaws that can cause insurers to go bust...

THE PREMIUM CYCLE

Insurance companies are particularly cyclical creatures, subject to a variety of in-built character flaws. First: the classic insurance cycle. This works thus: insurance company writes some business (i.e. sells a bunch of insurance policies), doesn't pay out that much in claims, makes an underwriting profit. So now it has a load of capital because it has the investment income from investing the premiums, plus an unexpected underwriting profit. It has to earn a return on that capital, so it tries to write more insurance business. But if last year was a good year for your accidents and claims, it was probably a good year for everyone. So everyone else is also trying to increase their market share. So these increasing volumes of business get written at decreasing or negative underwriting profits, and the insurance sector gets more and more dependent on investment income. Then a major disaster occurs – e.g. a big oil tanker sinks – and the company has to pay out huge sums in claims. Massive underwriting loss, massive erosion of capital (and therefore of future investment income), and nobody wants to write new business. This is actually the best time to be in the insurance industry (the year after a nice big hurricane or some such), because none of the big companies is trying to expand its market share, and you can write decent business at an underwriting profit.

So, for example, the CEO of Lloyd's of London, Nick Prettejohn, gave a superbly frank speech in 2005, which was a rallying call to the insurance industry to make an underwriting profit 'on more than an occasional basis'. He went on to say that the leading insurance companies should 'Stop destroying value'. In 2004, the UK insurance industry made an underwriting profit for the first time since 1978.

WRITE AND RUN

Warren Buffet holds much the same view, and whenever anyone will listen he points to the example of the National Indemnity Company in the US, which prides itself on not growing excessively and persistently making underwriting profits. The trouble is that another characteristic of the sector militates against such an approach being followed by many companies: the method by which bonuses are paid to underwriters. Essentially, they are rewarded by how much business they write, not how profitable it is. Moreover, since there is a clear time lag between selling an insurance policy and finding out how much money it has made the company – which for domestic insurance is up to a year, for commercial insurance can be much longer, and for life insurance can be decades long – in general, underwriters are bonused for a year's selling and then they can often move onto another job before they or the company ever finds out how much money they actually made.

This is known in the trade as the classic 'write and run' approach to insurance – write a load of business, get a bonus on the *estimated* profit, then run off to a better job before anyone finds out what the real profits were. Or indeed the losses.

IT'S THE BROKERS WHAT BROKE IT

The final characteristic of the insurance sector that accentuates its cyclical difficulties is the presence of brokers. Brokers perennially suffer from the crisis of confidence that leads them to believe that they will lose customers to other brokers who manage to keep get better deals from underwriters and undercut them. Hence, they permanently play insurers off against each other and try to get them to cut their prices for the trade they offer them. This especially happens during the underwriting good times when new insurance entrants enter the market and insurers have to cut prices in order to stay competitive. They do so, their business grows, and then bang – New Orleans' levees burst and the sector is in a world of pain again.

Spare a thought for the insurance industry. They do a

useful job, and they have a hellish time making money. But spare them just thoughts; when you're dealing with an insurance-type product, keep your hand on your wallet.

WHY DON'T MAINTENANCE MEN EVER TURN UP ON TIME?

In a moment of more than typical existential doubt, Woody Allen once said 'not only is there no God, try getting a plumber at weekends'. It's a notorious problem; unless you are prepared to pay massively over the odds, you're quite likely to find that your builders, plumbers and similar tradespeople don't necessarily always show up when they said they would, or at all. Is there a reason why that might be? Apart from the obvious ones that suggest themselves to you at 10.30am when you're sitting at home waiting for the no-show that you've taken a morning off work for.

Well, cheap lager and chaotic lifestyles are not entirely unknown as drivers of inefficiency in the building trades.

But even a syndicate of teetotal building monks would probably still have a lot of the same problems in showing up at correct times for their customers. The reason is because it's a scheduling problem, and scheduling problems are hard.

HURRY UP AND WAIT

Paint needs to dry, cement needs to set and parts, once ordered, need time to arrive. Some things can't be done in the rain. A certain proportion of the delays and hazards of the building trade are intrinsic to the business, even if they do sound like excuses. And it's the nature of the building industry that there's a logical order to things, which is pretty difficult to interrupt – you can't start work on the ceiling while you're waiting for the walls to be finished. And so any individual building project is going to have downtime built in the schedule – time when the builders are left with nothing to do, because the thing that comes next is dependent on something else that isn't finished yet and can't really be sped up.

SMALL IS PROBLEMATIC

On big building projects, this isn't much of a drag factor – big sites always have enough different things going on that there is some work that the idle hands can be put to while they're waiting. But on something like your new conservatory project, that's not the case. So, you can either literally pay for the builders to sit around doing nothing (that would be the 'way over the odds' option discussed earlier), or you can accept that they're often going to have more than one job on the go. The idea is that the spare periods of downtime fit into each other, and the less time-critical jobs can be scheduled around the more urgent ones.

THE TRAVELLING SALESMAN PROBLEM

The trouble is that it's like doing a jigsaw where the pieces keep changing size and shape. The normal random variation in any one component feeds into everything it depends on, and the system as a whole has a tendency to develop 'emergent' properties whereby delays snowball and seemingly minor setbacks have a huge knock-on effect. In general, scheduling problems are hard. The very simplest such problem is the 'Travelling Salesman Problem' with no uncertainty (for a given set of points on a map, find the shortest route that visits each of them exactly once), and mathematicians have actually proved that this has no simple formula for its solution and has to be worked out by trial and error.

NO SILVER BULLET

There are tricks of the trade and general principles that can be used to set up systems so that the inefficiencies caused by the uncertainty in scheduling problems is minimised, but there's no silver bullet. The field of study is called 'operations research' in business schools and 'cybernetics' in engineering schools, and anyone who can cope with the mathematics and the high level of abstraction involved can make a good career in optimising everything from air traffic control systems to the frequency with which ATMs are filled. But the basic principle is that the only sure way to damp down the feedback effects is to build a lot of 'slack' into the system; to ensure that, on average, each individual subsystem is working at well below maximum theoretical capacity, to allow for contingencies.

BUILDING IN THE SLACK

So, if you see your builders sitting around sipping cups of tea for the seventh time that day, seemingly doing nothing, don't immediately jump to the conclusion that you're being ripped off; it's possible that the 'slacking' that you see is literally that – an inevitable consequence of the tradeoff between maximising output and minimising the risk of a scheduling meltdown.

THE AFTERLIFE OF MONEY

THE BIG IDEAS OF ECONOMICS

And so we reach the end of this walk through money's secret life. We hope that through the journey you have picked up some of the Big Ideas of economics from the various different industries and sectors we have talked about. Perhaps now, when analysing a business you may say to yourself, 'Oh, this is like trade-show economics' rather than 'this is a network effect natural monopoly with high fixed and low marginal costs' as economists are wont to say. But, for the sake of completeness, and because different people think in different ways, here are what we think are the general principles that are worth thinking about when looking at the examples in this book.

THE COST OF BUSINESS

The first thing to look at when you are trying to understand what makes a business – any business – tick is what are their costs, and, specifically, what are their marginal costs. The marginal cost in a business is the cost of producing one more unit, or the cost that is saved by reducing output by one unit. This is not usually the same thing as the 'average cost', which is the total costs of the business (including overheads, CEO salary and all the other things that don't change depending on output) divided by the number of things produced. It's worth reading that one back once or twice as it's important – the difference between marginal and average costs is a big deal.

MARGINAL COST

The cost of making one more item, or providing one more hour of a service. In general, the change in cost for a small change in output. An important concept in economics, because there are good theoretical reasons to believe that the price of something will tend to settle down equal to its marginal cost.

ZERO OR VERY LOW MARGINAL COSTS

Economic textbooks are keen on showing examples where the marginal cost in a business is equal to or greater than the average cost. This is because they are going to take you down a road that leads to their favourite model of 'perfect competition'. Any economics textbook will show you why, in a perfectly competitive market, the price will tend to equal the marginal cost – basically, if the price is below the marginal cost, then the company is clearly going bust, as it makes a loss on every item. Whereas, if the price is above the marginal cost, there are some sales that could be profitably made but are being left on the table. Since there is so much pressure for the price to be roughly equal to the marginal cost, it matters a lot if this is very different from the average cost.

If the marginal cost (and therefore the price) is greater than the average cost, then you can be sure that the total money made from selling the goods (the price times the number of units sold) is going to be enough to cover the cost of making them all (which, by definition, is the average cost times the number of units sold). All fair enough. However, there are a *heck* of a lot of industries where the marginal cost is much less than the average; there are quite a few where the marginal cost is literally zero (electronic music downloads, for example).

And this is a problem. Because, snooty as we are about them, the models in the economics textbooks are basically right. There are always powerful competitive forces dragging pricing in the direction of marginal cost

– if nothing else, there is usually one big player in the industry which didn't like its market share last year. But if market cost is much lower than the average cost of producing the thing – usually because there are high fixed costs – then it's really dangerous to let the price fall anywhere near the marginal cost, because, if you do that, the total revenue (price times units) won't cover the overheads. In this case, marginal cost pricing isn't consistent with the industry continuing to exist!

Basically, lots of things that businesses do, which appear on the face of it to be weird, have their roots in an attempt to solve this problem. The basic problem of low marginal cost industries is that, because the marginal costs are low, people are always tempted to cut pricing in order to take market share, but this competitive urge has to be resisted because the price war would end up cutting everyone's margins so low that they would go out of business. In this situation, people start trying to find all sorts of grounds to compete on rather than price. Or the average firm size shrinks, so that they're not really competing with one another. Or they just learn to live with the periodic price wars and go out of business a lot (this seems to be what airlines do). Or the whole industry ends up being owned by the single lowest-cost producer, who then puts up their prices and earns a packet. There's a whole spectrum of outcomes that can be possible reactions but the underlying economic problem is the same.

RECURRING BUSINESS AND LONG-TERM RELATIONSHIPS

Economics textbooks always want to start you off thinking about anonymous, one-shot markets in which everyone deals with everyone else on equal terms and all the goods are as interchangeable as the money used to buy them. This misconception causes a reliable source of shock and disillusionment for young graduate trainees, as they emerge blinking and squealing into the business world to quickly discover that no two suppliers are ever exactly the same, and that specific personal relationships between specific people are the lifeblood of business.

The trouble is that in economics bygones are bygones, but in real life the decisions of the past are always hanging around. A customer base that's got used to one product won't always accept a supposedly interchangeable substitute. A machine that's been built with one kind of part can't be maintained with another. And, often most importantly, the supplier who you were with last year has spent that year *learning* about you and your business. Unless they are a powerful moron, they will have an advantage when it comes to making their pitch next year.

THE STICKINESS OF BUSINESS

Because of the stickiness of business, it's very rare that anyone makes a sale in the anticipation of never making a sale to that customer again. The people who do operate in such a world – such as estate agents, recruitment consultants, wedding planners – tend to have business practices that mark them out as rather unusual, shall we say. Lots of business activities that don't look like they make much sense when analysed on an economics textbook basis make a lot more sense when you think of them as part of an ongoing relationship.

LEAVE IT TO THE EXPERTS

Every industry, in our experience, has things in it that are easy enough to do *almost* right, and really difficult to do *just* right. Because of this, and unfortunately for anyone wanting an easy life, what tends to happen is that the players who do it 'just right' have a lower average and marginal cost than anybody else, so they can set the pricing at a level where they take as much market share as they can handle. And taking more market share tends to get them more economies of scale and more learning opportunities, making them even more of a problem for the rest of the industry. In a lot of contexts, good enough just isn't good enough.

HENCE HYPER-SPECIALISATION

It is because the very best players tend to have an advantage that grows over time that you often get hyper-specialisation in industries. For example, we once found out that, when dealing with garden centres, the plants that are sold to the customer have often travelled through three or four pairs of corporate hands before they reach the shopping trolley. It turns out that germinating seeds is one skill, growing the seedlings on to become immature plants is another, and thinning out the immature plants to get the viable ones that you see in the shops is yet a third. There are very few people or companies who can be the best at every single stage of the value chain, but plenty who can get close enough to the cutting edge at doing one particular thing. When you see an industry that is dis-aggregated, broken down into the constituent parts of the value chain, to what might otherwise seem a ludicrous degree, this is usually why.

THE SECRET

Economics is a complicated discipline, and the way actual economies work is even more complex. Businesses act in what appear to be illogical and inconsistent ways, due to sticky relationships, quest for market share, and many other factors. Implementing the theory of hyper-specialisation would suggest that to fully understand the changing dynamics in one sector is a challenge, but for any one individual to fully understand those of every sector in the modern economy is a near impossibility. But we like to live dangerously, so we hope to have succeeded in adding a little knowledge around the margins.

GLOSSARY OF
KEY TERMS

Amortised – 1. The original sense of 'amortise' is the gradual repayment of a debt in instalments, as opposed to in one lump at the end. 2. Figuratively, based on this, any sort of 'spreading out' over time; so, in accountant speak, non-physical assets like brands and contracts are 'amortised' rather than 'depreciated'. 3. Even more figuratively, any sort of 'spreading out' at all; so one might talk about research expenditure being 'amortised' over a large production run, which would obviously be more efficient than a small one for this reason.

Bonds – a bond is a tradeable loan issued by a company or a government. Company bonds are a way of raising money for a company – rather than borrowing money from the bank, the company sells IOUs to the public.

Cartel – an agreement between companies in an industry to fix prices, usually by keeping supply lower than the amount that could really be produced. The practice is usually illegal.

Credit default swap – this is a derivatives contract that pays out a sum of money if a particular company defaults on its debt.

Depreciation – an item in a company's accounts that allows for the fact that the assets will have lost value over a year simply because they are one year older. A familiar concept to buyers of new sports cars.

Depreciation life – usually, the depreciation on an asset is calculated by estimating its useful life, and deducting a proportion of its value every year until it is 'fully depreciated'. The depreciation life is only ever a rough estimate, and companies often choose to use substantially shorter estimates than the real useful life, because this lets them take a bigger charge (which is deductible from profits for tax purposes, even though it's not an item of cash you need to pay)

Economies of scale – some things are just more efficient to make in big units or large production runs. You can gain benefits of mass production (like Henry Ford) or spread out the fixed costs of making specialised tools. So, as your 'scale' increases, your average cost per unit falls. At some point, all the economies of scale are used up, and bigger production facilities become inefficient, as they need more management and overhead – this is why you sometimes hear about 'diseconomies of scale'.

Exposure – the total amount that somebody (or some company, or some government) owes to you is your 'exposure' to that 'counterparty'. It's the maximum amount you stand to lose if they go bust.

Foreclosure – to foreclose on a company is to declare it bankrupt, then move in and take ownership of the assets to try to get back some of the money it owes you. There are fairly complicated rules about who is allowed to foreclose, what they are allowed to do with the assets and what agreements they have to get from other creditors.

Fungibility – a piece of financial jargon effectively meaning that two bits of paper are interchangeable. Pound notes are fungible – it doesn't matter which particular one you have. So are most shares. Bonds, however, are not necessarily fungible – different bonds have different maturities and interest payments. In the world of physical objects, hammers and shovels are pretty fungible – wedding rings, decidedly less so.

Leverage – the amount of debt that a company (or some other project) has. The analogy is to mechanical leverage because it increases the profits if things go right (you only have to pay back the debt, you don't have to share the upside), but increases the losses if they don't (you still have to pay back the debt if you don't make any profits at all).

Marginal cost – the cost of making one more item, or providing one more hour of a service. In general, the change in cost for a small change in output. An important concept in economics, because there are good theoretical reasons to believe that the price of something will tend to settle down equal to its marginal cost.

Short position – effectively, 'betting' that the price of a share will go down. The way this is achieved is to borrow the share and sell it, in the hope that, when you have to return the share, you will be able to buy it back in the market for a lower price.